Doing Quantitative Research in Education
with SPSS

Daniel Muijs

Sage Publications
London • Thousand Oaks • New Delhi

SAGE Publications Ltd
1 Oliver's Yard
55 City Road
London EC1Y 1SP

SAGE Publications Inc.
2455 Teller Road
Thousand Oaks, California 91320

SAGE Publications India Pvt Ltd
B-42, Panchsheel Enclave
Post Box 4109
New Delhi 100 017

British Library Cataloguing in Publication data

A catalogue record for this book is available from the British Library

ISBN 0-7619-4382-X
ISBN 0-7619-4383-8 (pbk)

Library of Congress Control Number: 2003115358

Typeset by Pantek Arts Ltd
Printed in Great Britain by Athenaeum Press Ltd, Gateshead, Tyne & Wear

Contents

List of figures

List of tables

Preface

In this book we will be looking at quantitative research methods in education. The book is structured to start with chapters on conceptual issues and designing quantitative research studies before going on to data analysis. While each chapter can be studied separately, a better understanding will be reached by reading the book sequentially.

This book is intended as a non-mathematical introduction, and a software package will be used to analyse the data. This package is SPSS, the most commonly used statistical software package in the social sciences. A dataset from which all examples are taken can be downloaded from the accompanying website (www.sagepub.co.uk/resources/muijs.htm). The website also contains the answers to the exercises at the end of each chapter, additional teaching resources (to be added over time), and a facility to address questions and feedback to the author.

I hope you find this book useful, and above all that it will give you the confidence to conduct and interpret the results of your own quantitative inquiries in education.

Daniel Muijs

▪ ▪ ▪ Chapter 1

Introduction to qu: research

▪ ▪ ▪ What is quantitative research?

Research methods in education (and the other social sciences) are often divided into two main types: quantitative and qualitative methods. This book will discuss one of these two main strands: quantitative methods. In this chapter we will have a look at what is meant by the term quantitative methods, and what distinguishes quantitative from qualitative methods.

When you think of quantitative methods, you will probably have specific things in mind. You will probably be thinking of statistics, numbers – many of you may be feeling somewhat apprehensive because you think quantitative methods are difficult. Apart from the last, all these thoughts capture some of the essence of quantitative methods.

The following definition, taken from Aliaga and Gunderson (2002), describes what we mean by quantitative research methods very well:

> Quantitative research is 'Explaining phenomena by collecting numerical data that are analysed using mathematically based methods (in particular statistics).'

Let's go through this definition step by step. The first element is *explaining phenomena*. This is a key element of all research, be it quantitative or qualitative. When we set out do some research, we are always looking to explain something. In education this could be questions like 'why do teachers leave teaching?', 'what factors influence pupil achievement?' and so on.

The specificity of quantitative research lies in the next part of the definition. In quantitative research we collect *numerical data*. This is closely connected to the final part of the definition: analysis *using mathematically*

1

ds. In order to be able to use mathematically based methods our *e* to be in numerical form. This is not the case for qualitative *h*. Qualitative data are not necessarily or usually numerical, and *efore* cannot be analysed using statistics.

Therefore, because quantitative research is essentially about collecting numerical data to explain a particular phenomenon, particular questions seem immediately suited to being answered using quantitative methods:

- How many males get a first-class degree at university compared to females?
- What percentage of teachers and school leaders belong to ethnic minority groups?
- Has pupil achievement in English improved in our school district over time?

These are all questions we can look at quantitatively, as the data we need to collect are already available to us in numerical form. However, does this not severely limit the usefulness of quantitative research? There are many phenomena we might want to look at, but which don't seem to produce any quantitative data. In fact, relatively few phenomena in education actually occur in the form of 'naturally' quantitative data.

Luckily, we are far less limited than might appear from the above. Many data that do not naturally appear in quantitative form can be collected in a quantitative way. We do this by designing research instruments aimed specifically at converting phenomena that don't naturally exist in quantitative form into quantitative data, which we can analyse statistically. Examples of this are attitudes and beliefs. We might want to collect data on pupils' attitudes to their school and their teachers. These attitudes obviously do not naturally exist in quantitative form (we don't form our attitudes in the shape of numerical scales!). Yet we can develop a questionnaire that asks pupils to rate a number of statements (for example, 'I think school is boring') as either agree strongly, agree, disagree or disagree strongly, and give the answers a number (e.g. 1 for disagree strongly, 4 for agree strongly). Now we have quantitative data on pupil attitudes to school. In the same way, we can collect data on a wide number of phenomena, and make them quantitative through data collection instruments like questionnaires or tests. In the next three chapters we will look at how we can develop instruments to do just that.

The number of phenomena we can study in this way is almost unlimited, making quantitative research quite flexible. However, not all phenomena are best studied using quantitative methods. As we will see, while quantitative methods have some notable advantages, they also have disadvantages, which means that some phenomena are better studied using different (qualitative) methods.

The last part of the definition refers to the use of *mathematically based methods*, in particular *statistics*, to analyse the data. This is what people usually think about when they think of quantitative research, and is often seen as the most important part of quantitative studies. This is a bit of a misconception. While it is important to use the right data analysis tools, it is even more important to use the right research design and data collection instruments. However, the use of statistics to analyse the data is the element that puts a lot of people off doing quantitative research, because the mathematics underlying the methods seem complicated and frightening. Nevertheless, as we will see later on in this book, most researchers do not really have to be particularly expert in the mathematics underlying the methods, because computer software allows us to do the analyses quickly and (relatively) easily.

■ ■ ■ Foundations of quantitative research methods

Realism, subjectivism and the 'paradigm wars'

Now we have defined quantitative research, let's compare it with qualitative research, against which it is usually contrasted. While quantitative research is based on numerical data analysed statistically, qualitative research uses non-numerical data. Qualitative research is actually an umbrella term encompassing a wide range of methods, such as interviews, case studies, ethnographic research and discourse analysis, to name just a few examples.

The difference between quantitative and qualitative research is often seen as quite fundamental, leading people to talk about 'paradigm wars' in which quantitative and qualitative research are seen as belligerent and incompatible factions (a bit like capitalism and communism). Many researchers define themselves as either quantitative or qualitative. Where does this idea come from?

This idea is linked to what are seen as the different underlying philosophies and worldviews of researchers in the two 'paradigms' (also called 'epistemologies'). According to this view, two fundamentally different worldviews underlie quantitative and qualitative research. The quantitative view is described as being 'realist' or sometimes 'positivist', while the worldview underlying qualitative research is viewed as being 'subjectivist'.

What does this mean? Realists take the view that what research does is uncover an existing reality. 'The truth is out there' and it is the job of the researcher to use objective research methods to uncover that truth. This means that the researcher needs to be as detached from the research as possible, and use methods that maximise objectivity and minimise the involvement of the researcher in the research. This is best done using methods taken largely from the natural sciences (e.g. biology, physics, etc.), which are then transposed to social research settings (like education). Positivism is the most extreme form of this worldview. According to positivism, the world works according to fixed laws of cause and effect. Scientific thinking is used to test theories about these laws, and either reject or provisionally accept them. In this way, we will finally get to understand the truth about how the world works. By developing reliable measurement instruments, we can objectively study the physical world.

However, this view, that there is a true reality out there that we can measure completely objectively, is problematic. We are all part of the world we are observing, and cannot completely detach ourselves from what we are researching. Historical research has shown that what is studied and what findings are produced are influenced by the beliefs of the people doing the research and the political/social climate at the time the research is done.

If one looks at research from a quantitative versus qualitative perspective, qualitative researchers are subjectivists. In contrast to the realist view that the truth is out there and can be objectively measured and found through research, subjectivists point to the role of human subjectivity in the process of research. Reality is not 'out there' to be objectively and dispassionately observed by us, but is at least in part constructed by us and by our observations. There is no pre-existing objective reality that can be observed. The process of our observing reality changes and transforms it, and therefore subjectivists are relativistic. All truth can only be relative and is never definitive as the positivists claim. The extreme relativist position is obviously as problematic as the extreme positivistic one, because, for example, it would in theory deny that anything more than social con-sensus and power distinguishes witchcraft and modern science.

If you look at the extreme forms of the two views we have set out here, it would seem that quantitative and qualitative research methods are pretty incompatible. These extremes are, however, a gross simplification of the views of both quantitative and qualitative researchers, and very few people in either 'camp' subscribe to them. I have included them here because they are frequently presented in only slightly less extreme forms as straw men with which critics of one method (qualitative for example) may attack users of different methods (for example quantitative). Qualitative methods is an umbrella term for a large number of different research methods (such as participant observation, interviews, case stud-ies, ethnographic research) which are quite different. They are used by researchers with quite different worldviews, some of which clearly lie towards the realistic end of the spectrum. To ascribe radical subjectivist views to all qualitative researchers is a fallacy.

To label all quantitative researchers positivists is equally inaccurate. Quantitative researchers have taken up many criticisms of positivist views, and there are now a variety of epistemologies underlying theory and practice in quantitative research. I think it is true to say that very few quantitative researchers nowadays are radical positivists.

Post-positivism, experiential realism and pragmatism

Post-positivists accept the critique of traditional positivism that has been presented by the subjectivists, without going so far as to reject any notion of realism. Post-positivists accept that we cannot observe the world we are part of as totally objective and disinterested outsiders, and accept that the natural sciences do not provide the model for all social research. However, they do believe in the possibility of an objective real-ity. While we will never be able to totally uncover that reality through our research, post-positivists believe that we should try and approximate that reality as best we can, all the while realising that our own subjectiv-ity is shaping that reality. Rather than finding the truth, the post-positivist will try and represent reality as best he or she can.

In contrast to positivists, post-positivists believe that research can never be certain. Rather than focusing on certainty and absolute truth, post-positivist social science focuses on confidence – how much can we rely on our findings? how well do they predict certain outcomes?

A second worldview or epistemology that underlies the work of some quantitative researchers is called *experiential realism*. Experiential realism claims, as do anti-positivist positions, that we cannot observe the world in a purely objective way, because our perception itself influences what we see and measure. In contrast to subjectivist positions, however, experiential realists believe that there is a limit to subjectivity. Humans are limited in their subjectivity by the fact that we use a limited number of schemas to formulate our views of the world. This is because our perception is 'embodied'. We don't observe passively, but actively interact with the world through our bodies.

Experiential realists see the use of metaphor as crucial to the way we make sense of the world around us. We use metaphors to understand our world. One of the main metaphors we use to do this is the subject/object schema, which divides the world up into objects (things) and subjects (people). This metaphor has its origins in the fact that in our dealings with the world we find that there is a distinction between an external world consisting of edges, surfaces and textures that are not us, and those things that are us, the actor. As we move around our world, the objects remain invariant. Science, according to this view, is an activity that is based on this subject/object schema (Mulaik, 1995).

A lot of researchers, both quantitative and qualitative (the author included), take a pragmatist approach to research, using different methods depending on the research question they are trying to answer. In some cases this will lead them to quantitative research, for example when they need to give a quantitative answer to a question or generalise findings to a population, or are looking to test a theory mathematically; in other cases they will employ qualitative methods. Sometimes a mixed methods approach combining quantitative and qualitative methods will be the most appropriate.

Philosophers like Peirce, Dewey and James developed pragmatism as a philosophy in the USA. One of the main contentions of this school of philosophy is that the meaning and the truth of any idea is a function of its practical outcome(s). Pragmatists strongly oppose the absolutism they see as a key part of most other philosophical beliefs, and put themselves in opposition to other philosophies (think of the positivist/subjectivist debate) which are totally rejected.

As for the subjectivists, there is no definite truth in pragmatic philosophy. Truth is constantly changing and being updated through the process of human problem-solving. The key question for pragmatists is not 'is it true?' or 'is it right?' but 'does it work?'

■ ■ ■ When do we use quantitative methods?

If we take a pragmatic approach to research methods, first of all we need to find out what kinds of questions are best answered using quantitative as opposed to qualitative methods.

There are four main types of research question that quantitative research is particularly suited to find an answer to:

1. The first is when we want a quantitative answer. Examples are: 'How many students choose to study education?' or 'How many mathematics teachers do we need and how many have we got in our school district?' That we need to use quantitative research to answer this kind of question is obvious. Qualitative, non-numerical methods will obviously not provide us with the (numerical) answer we want.

2. Numerical change can likewise only accurately be studied using quantitative methods. Are the numbers of students in our university rising or falling? Is achievement going up or down? We would need to do a quantitative study to find out.

3. As well as wanting to find out about the state of something, we often want to explain phenomena. What factors predict the recruitment of mathematics teachers? What factors are related to changes in student achievement over time? As we will see later in this book, this kind of question can also be studied successfully using quantitative methods, and many statistical techniques have been developed that allow us to predict scores on one factor or *variable* (e.g. teacher recruitment) from scores on one or more other factors or *variables* (e.g. unemployment rates, pay, conditions).

4. The final activity for which quantitative research is especially suited is the testing of *hypotheses*. We might want to explain something, for example whether there is a relationship between a pupil's achievement and their self-esteem and social background.

We could look at the theory and come up with the hypothesis that lower social class background leads to low self-esteem, which would in turn be related to low achievement. Using quantitative research we can try and test this kind of model.

■ ■ ■ Units and variables

When we collect data in quantitative educational research, we have to collect them from someone or something. The people or things (e.g. schools) we collect data on or from are known as *units* or *cases*.

The data that we are collecting from these units are known as *variables*. Variables are any characteristic of the unit we are interested in and want to collect (e.g. gender, age, self-esteem).

The name variable refers to the fact that this data will differ between units. For example, achievement will differ between pupils and schools, gender will differ between pupils, and so on. If there are no differences at all between units we want to study we probably aren't going to be able to do any interesting research (for example, studying whether pupils are human would not yield interesting findings).

■ ■ ■ What is a hypothesis?

A hypothesis is a tentative explanation that accounts for a set of facts and can be tested by further investigation.

For example, one hypothesis we might want to test could be that poverty causes low achievement, or that there is a relationship between pupils' self-esteem and the amount of time they spend watching television.

Quantitative researchers will design studies that allow us to test these hypotheses. We will collect the relevant data (for example, parental income and school achievement) and use statistical techniques to decide whether or not to reject or provisionally accept the hypothesis.

Accepting a hypothesis is always provisional, as new data may emerge that causes it to be rejected later on.

The types of problem outlined in 1 and 2 opposite are called 'descriptive' – we are merely trying to describe a situation – while those in 3 and 4 are 'inferential' – we are trying to explain something rather than just describe it.

As mentioned above, while quantitative methods are good at answering these four types of questions, there are other types of question that are not well suited to quantitative methods:

1. The first situation where quantitative research will fail is when we want to explore a problem in depth. Quantitative research is good at providing information in breadth from a large number of units. But when we want to explore a problem or concept in depth quantitative methods are too shallow. To really get under the skin of a phenomenon, we will need to go for ethnographic methods, interviews, in-depth case studies and other qualitative techniques.

2. We saw above that quantitative research is well-suited for the testing of theories and hypotheses. What quantitative methods cannot do very well is develop hypotheses and theories. The hypotheses to be tested may come from a review of the literature or theory, but can also be developed using exploratory qualitative research.

3. If issues to be studied are particularly complex, an in-depth qualitative study (a case study, for example) is more likely to pick up on this than a quantitative study. This is partly because there is a limit to how many variables can be looked at in any one quantitative study, and partly because in quantitative research it is the researcher who defines the variables to be studied. In qualitative research unexpected variables may emerge.

4. Finally, while quantitative methods are better at looking at cause and effect (causality, as it is known), qualitative methods are more suited to looking at the meaning of particular events or circumstances.

What then do we do if we want to look at both breadth and depth, or at both causality and meaning? In these situations, it is best to use a so-called *mixed methods* design in which we use both quantitative (for example, a questionnaire) and qualitative (for example, a number of case studies) methods. Mixed methods research is a flexible approach where the research design is determined by what we want to find out rather than by any predetermined epistemological position. In mixed methods research, qualitative or quantitative components can predominate or both can have equal status.

▪ ▪ ▪ Common misconceptions

1. *I have to have an epistemology to do research, don't I?* No, not necessarily. While you may have strong epistemological and philosophical beliefs that determine what kind of research you want to do, you can also start out wanting to solve a particular problem or wanting to find out about a particular phenomenon. In such a situation you will be able to pragmatically choose what methods are best suited to solving your research question.

2. *Data has to be in a quantitative format to do quantitative research, doesn't it?* Not necessarily. If data are not naturally available as numbers, you can try and turn non-quantitative data (like attitudes or opinions) into quantitative data by measuring them numerically (for example, by using a questionnaire rating scale).

3. *Qualitative and quantitative research are incompatible, aren't they?* Not necessarily. Qualitative and quantitative research can be usefully combined in mixed methods designs, which often produce a lot of useful information. Also, depending on your research question, you might in one instance want to use quantitative and in another instance qualitative research. This is something I personally often do.

4. *The most important thing about quantitative research is the statistics, isn't it?* Not at all. While the way in which you analyse your data matters, if you haven't designed your research well and collected the data in a valid and reliable way, you will not get valid results however sophisticated your analyses.

5. *Qualitative research is purely subjective, isn't it?* Not necessarily. While some qualitative researchers might take a strong subjectivist stance, there is a wide variety of qualitative methods that can accommodate a variety of viewpoints.

6. *We can never explain things using quantitative research. To do that we need to use qualitative methods.* That is not strictly true. While qualitative research usually provides more depth and less breadth than quantitative research, a well-designed quantitative study will allow us not just to look at what happens, but to provide an explanation of why it happens as well. The key lies in your research design and what variables you collect.

■ ■ ■ Summary

In this chapter we have discussed what quantitative research is. We said quantitative research is about explaining phenomena by collecting quantitative data which are analysed using mathematically based methods.

The fact that the data have to be quantitative does not mean that they have to be naturally available in quantitative form. Non-quantitative phenomena (such as teacher beliefs) can be turned into quantitative data through our measurement instruments.

Quantitative research is often placed in opposition to qualitative research. This is often turned into a 'paradigm war' which is seen to result from apparently incompatible worldviews underlying the methods. When you look closer at researchers' actual beliefs, it appears that the so-called subjectivist (qualitative) versus realist (quantitative) divide is not that clear-cut.

Many researchers take a pragmatic approach to research and use quantitative methods when they are looking for breadth, want to test a hypothesis or want to study something quantitative. If they are looking for depth and meaning, they will prefer to use qualitative methods. In many cases, mixed methods approaches will be appropriate.

■ ■ ■ Exercises

1. Gender (male/female) is not a quantitative variable. Can you think of any ways you could study gender in quantitative research?

2. Learning styles (e.g. visual, audio, kinaesthetic) are not a quantitative variable. Can you think of any ways you could study learning styles in quantitative research?

3. What is your worldview (epistemology) with regard to research? Do you think it is compatible with using quantitative methods?

4. Can you think of a research question you could study using quantitative methods?

5. What kind of research question would you study using a mixed methods design?

6. What are the main distinctions between post-positivism and positivism?

■ ■ ■ Further reading

If you want to know more about quantitative and qualitative research, a good overview of a range of methods is given in Cohen, L., Manion, L. and Morison, K. (2000) *Research Methods in Education*, 5th edn (Routledge Falmer). This also gives an introduction to the subjectivist–realist epistemological debate.

An excellent introduction to mixed methodology research is Tashakkori, A. and Teddlie, C. (2000) *Mixed Methodology* (Sage Publications).

A fascinating but tough work by a leading proponent of experiential realism is Lakoff, G. (1990) *Women, Fire and Dangerous Things. What Categories of Thought Reveal About the Mind* (University of Chicago Press).

Menand, L. (ed.) (1998) *Pragmatism* (Random House), is a selection of writings by pragmatist philosophers, old and new, and is probably the best overview of this philosophy around.

■ ■ ■ Chapter 2

Experimental and quasi-experimental research

■ ■ ■ Types of quantitative research

Once you have taken the decision to do a quantitative study, you have to design it. There are two main types of quantitative research design, *experimental* designs and *non-experimental* designs. Experimental designs are sometimes known as 'the scientific method' due to their popularity in scientific research where they originated. Non-experimental research is sometimes (wrongly, as we will see in the next chapter) equated with survey research and is very common in the social sciences.

When hearing the term experimental designs, most of us think back to school experiments in science. Experimental research in the social sciences follows the same basic pattern as those (natural) science experiments.

The basis of the experimental method is the experiment, which can be defined as: *a test under controlled conditions that is made to demonstrate a known truth or examine the validity of a hypothesis.* The key element of this definition is *control*, and that is where experimental research differs from non-experimental quantitative research. When doing an experiment we want to control the environment as much as possible and only concentrate on those variables that we want to study. This is why experiments traditionally take place in laboratories, environments where all extraneous influences can be shut out. In non-experimental research we will not be able to control out extraneous influences. Control is also increased by the fact that in an experiment the researcher manipulates the variable that is supposed to affect the outcome of the experiment, the so-called *predictor* variable, while in non-experimental research we have to use the variable 'as it appears' in practice.

■ ■ ■ Example 2.1

Violent attitudes and deferred academic aspirations: deleterious effects of exposure to rap music

In this study, a team from the University of North Carolina (Johnson, Jackson and Gatto, 1995) sought to look at the effects of watching violent rap music videos (experimental group), compared to non-violent rap music videos (control group 1) or no music videos (control group 2) on adolescents' attitudes to violence and deviant behaviour. Forty-six 11–16-year-old boys from a club in Wilmington were randomly assigned to one of the three conditions. In the violent condition, subjects were shown eight videos containing violent images. Those in the non-violent condition were shown eight non-violent videos. Following the viewing, subjects were asked to read a text passage in which a boy hit another boy who kissed his girlfriend and respond to a number of questions on the acceptability of this behaviour. After that, they read another text passage, featuring a discussion between two characters. One had a 'nice car' and 'nice clothes' through dodgy activities while the other was completing college. Subjects were then asked to respond to a number of questions probing their views of these alternative career choices. The control (non-video) group also participated in this activity. Subjects were told that the videos were part of a memory test and had been randomly chosen. Results showed that the subjects exposed to the videos were significantly more likely to approve of violent behaviour and of a deviant career path than those who viewed the non-violent video. The controls were least likely to approve of violence or a deviant career path.

This experiment suggests a deleterious effect of watching violent videos. However, a number of caveats need to be taken into account. Firstly, as mentioned above, this is clearly a somewhat contrived situation. It is not clear from this experiment how strong this effect is, and therefore whether it is practically significant within a real-life context in which many other factors may affect attitudes to violence. The sample is from a very specific group (black boys from a boys club), and the extent to which these findings generalise to other populations needs to be examined. The authors also did not provide any information on prior factors that could differ between the groups (e.g. age), notwithstanding random assignment to groups. This study therefore would need replication in further experiments before we could say anything definitive, although the findings are clearly of great interest.

■ ■ ■ How to design an experimental study

There are a number a number of steps to go through when doing experimental research. These are outlined in the following sections.

Define your research objectives

Any research design starts with formulating the research objectives. This step needs to be taken *before* you decide whether or not to do experimental research, as the research objectives will determine what kind of research to do. Your research objectives describe what you want to study and how. You need to spell out clearly what the aims of your research are. Research objectives need to be realistic. It is important to understand that you can't do everything. We have to limit ourselves to what is actually researchable. For example, let's say we want to look at the effects of different test conditions on examination performance. When we think this through, there are an almost unlimited number of conditions that could vary slightly and affect test performance, such as lighting levels, how many adults are present, seating arrangements, temperature and so on. To look at all of these in one study would be impractical and all but impossible. So we will need to set ourselves a more limited goal, by thinking about which aspects might really make a difference and choosing just one (or a small number), for example seating arrangements. Our research objective would then be to look at whether or not seating arrangements affect examination performance.

We also need to be clear on what our *population* is. The population is the group of people we want to *generalise* to. For example, if we were to do this experiment, we would use, say, 40 students in two different seating arrangements and see what effects we can find. Usually, we don't just want to draw conclusions that are only applicable to that group of 40 students. What we want to do is say something about seating arrangements among students more generally. Many statistical methods that we will discuss in the following chapters have been designed to allow us to do just that. But before we can do this, we must be clear about which population we actually want to generalise to. All students of 18 and over? First-years only? This is important because it will affect who we get to take part in our experiment. If I did a study using only secondary school kids, I couldn't then go out and generalise to primary age kids.

Formulate hypotheses

The research objectives you have developed now need to be refined into the form of a number of specific research hypotheses you want to test. A research *hypothesis* can be defined as 'a tentative explanation that accounts for a set of facts and can be tested by further investigation', as we mentioned earlier. In experimental research, we traditionally look at two distinct types of hypotheses: the *null hypothesis* and the *alternative hypothesis*. The alternative hypothesis is the one we want to be true, the null hypothesis is the opposite. For example, I might want to know whether adding moving pictures to a presentation will improve pupils' memory of the key content of the presentation. I would have two hypotheses:

- Null hypothesis (H_0): adding moving pictures will *not* improve pupils' retention of the content.
- Alternative hypothesis (H_1): adding moving pictures *will* improve pupils' retention of the content.

This example presents the most simple case, where there is only one hypothesis to be tested. In many studies there will be several hypotheses, and one can also hypothesise *mediating* factors that influence the relationship between the variables. An additional hypothesis that includes as a mediating factor whether or not moving pictures are aligned to content could be:

- H_1: adding moving pictures will improve pupils' retention of content *if* the moving pictures are closely aligned to the content.
- H_0: adding moving pictures will not improve pupils' retention of content *if* the moving pictures are not closely aligned to the content.

While the terminology refers to a 'null hypothesis', this does not necessarily mean that the null hypothesis always has to specify that there is not going to be any effect while the alternative hypothesis specifies that there will be an effect. The null hypothesis can itself predict a specific value, for example:

- H_1: the difference between boys and girls on a word retention test will be more than 20 per cent.
- H_0: the difference between boys and girls on a word retention will be less than 20 per cent.

or:

- H_1: the mean score on a self-esteem inventory will be between 20 and 30.
- H_0: the mean score on a self-esteem inventory will be between 10 and 20.

In practice, most researchers test a null hypothesis of no difference because standard statistical tests are usually designed to test just that hypothesis. However, it is important to remember that other types of null hypothesis are possible, because a value or difference of zero might not be realistic for the research question you are looking at.

▬▬▬ Example 2.2

How should verbal information be presented to students to enhance learning from animations: auditorily as speech or visually as on-screen text?

This question was studied by Mayer and Moreno (1998), who conducted an experiment in which students were asked to view an animation showing the process of lightning either accompanied by concurrent narration or on-screen text. The theory they wanted to test was that visual and auditory learning are processed in two different parts of the working memory: the visual working memory and the auditory working memory. That would mean that if narration is given alongside the animation, students will represent the narration and animation in two different parts of the working memory, while if on-screen text is presented with animation, students will try to represent both the animation and text in the same part of memory (the visual auditory memory) which may then become overloaded. Better performance was therefore hypothesised for the text group.

The experiment was conducted by randomly assigning students to the two groups, one viewing the narration with on-screen text, the other with narration. Following the presentation, students were given a retention, matching and transfer test. It was found that students in the animation–narration group did significantly better than those in the animation–text group on all three tests, supporting the experimenters' hypothesis.

Set up your research design

Once one or more hypotheses have been set up, you need to decide how to test these hypotheses. If an experimental methodology is chosen (the advantages and disadvantages will be discussed in the next section of this chapter), you will then have to decide what experimental design to use.

The traditional experimental design, known as the *pre-test post-test control group design* works as follows: participants (often known as 'subjects' in experimental research) are placed into two groups, the experimental and the control group. The experimental group will receive the 'treatment' (e.g. watching a violent music video as in Example 2.1 p.14), the control group will not. Both groups will receive a pre-test on whatever instrument is used to assess the effect of the experiment (e.g. a test) before the treatment is given, and a post-test, usually on the same instrument, after the treatment has been given. The sequence therefore is:

	1. Pre-test	2. Treatment	3. Post-test
Experimental group	X	X	X
Control group	X		X

Following the post-test, statistical analyses are carried out to see whether the treatment has had an effect (see later).

There are a number of variations on this basic design. As we have seen in Example 2.2, it is often desirable to have more than one treatment group. There can, for example, be variations in the treatment that we might want to study. In Example 2.2 (see box) we have two treatment groups and one control group. More control groups and treatment groups are also possible. The pre-test post-test design is also not always followed, as we can see in Example 2.1 where no pre-test is used. Usually it is better to use both a pre- and a post-test, though, because without pre-testing we can never be sure that any difference we find on the post-test is the result of the treatment and not the result of differences that already existed between the two groups before the treatment.

Another decision you will have to take is whether or not to give the control group a *placebo*. This practice comes from medical research, where it is well-known that some patients show recovery as a result of a belief in the treatment rather than as a result of the treatment itself.

Because of this, it is common practice in medical trials to provide the control group with a placebo treatment (for example, a sugar pill) rather than nothing at all. Often, a percentage of the group given a sugar pill will show recovery as a result of their belief that they are taking an effective pill. This obviously means that if no placebo was given, we couldn't say for certain whether any effect of the treatment was because it actually worked or because some patients believed it works. This can be an issue in educational research as well.

That individual behaviours may be altered because participants in the study know they are being studied was demonstrated in a research project (1927–32) which looked at raising worker productivity in a factory. This series of studies, first led by Harvard Business School professor Elton Mayo along with associates F. J. Roethlisberger and William J. Dickson, started out by examining the physical and environmental influences of the workplace (e.g. brightness of lights, humidity) and later moved on to the psychological aspects (e.g. breaks, group pressure, working hours, managerial leadership). One of the main findings was that productivity increased regardless of the innovation introduced. One explanation is that this is the result of the extra attention paid to the workers (by the researchers) which motivated them to work harder. The same effect could also occur in educational settings. An intervention, for example a programme to help improve pupils' reading skills, could motivate pupils because of the additional attention they are receiving, leading to higher achievement. Likewise, when teachers engage in a new project, they may work harder and be more motivated simply because they are doing something new or because they know they are part of a research study.

Selecting a placebo can be hard in educational experiments, though. It is not as simple as giving patients a sugar pill. Any placebo intervention has to be sufficiently plausible to have an effect, and therefore is often likely to become an intervention in itself. This causes two problems: firstly the additional cost and effort involved in developing a plausible placebo, and secondly the fact that we are now measuring the effect of one treatment against that of another treatment rather than against a control! Therefore, in these cases it can often be a good idea to have two control groups: a 'placebo' group (which receives a placebo intervention) and a 'real' control group (which doesn't receive any intervention). In some cases schools have been given money to buy in any intervention they want rather than the researchers developing a second intervention themselves.

Select instruments

Once you have selected a suitable experimental design, you need to select or develop appropriate pre- and post-test measures. This is crucially important, as neither a high-quality experimental design nor sophisticated statistical analyses can make up for bad measurement. In just the same way a carpenter also needs proper tools – imagine trying to build a car with a hammer, some nails and a plank of wood and you will see what I mean! The measurement instruments must first of all measure what we want them to. This is known as *validity*. Secondly, our instrument must be *reliable*. Validity and reliability are discussed in Chapter 4.

Select appropriate levels at which to test your hypotheses

In an experimental design you will have to think carefully about the right level of treatment at which to test your hypothesis. The importance of this becomes clear when you think of the medicine paracetamol. The right dosage can stop headaches and pains. Too little will not have any effect, too much will kill you. While the consequences of too much educational intervention are usually less serious, getting the 'dosage' right is nonetheless important. Think of a programme that provides extra support in reading to students who are behind their reading age. If too little extra support is provided, it may not have the desired effect. If too much support is provided, students may become bored and disaffected with the programme, or improvements in reading may come at the expense of other subjects like mathematics.

In some cases you might want to test the effect of different levels of the treatment. If you look at Example 2.2 (see box), would it make a difference how much text is added to the animation as to whether or not this treatment leads to positive results? In that case a series of experiments can be carried out varying the level of treatment given to the experimental group.

Assign persons to groups

Assigning persons to groups is the next stage in the experimental design. As we mentioned above, in experimental research we are always trying to minimise the influence of any external factors. This means that we want to ensure that the experimental and control group differ as little as possible at the start of the experiment. Otherwise any effect we might find might be caused by differences between people in the groups rather than by the treatment. Imagine, for example, that in Example 2.2 we had selected students from a high set class to be in the animation–narration group, and students from the lower set to be in the animation–text group. The differences found on the tests would then be likely to be the result of the fact that the animation–narration group were academically higher performers rather than being the result of narration being a more effective accompaniment for animation than text. Therefore, we want there to be no bias in our assignment of people to groups.

The best way to achieve this is through *randomisation*. This means that once we have selected subjects to take part in our study, they are randomly assigned to either the control or experimental group, for example by giving everyone a number and then randomly selecting numbers to be part of either the experimental or the control group. Randomisation is most likely to ensure that there is no bias as everyone will have an exactly equal chance to be in each group. The effect is essentially similar to playing a card game with two people. By shuffling the cards and dividing them, we are ensuring that every card has an equal chance of ending up with each player. Obviously, we do need to have a sufficiently large group of people to make randomisation work.

In order to test whether this has been successful, it is good practice to collect data on each participant on any variable that you think might affect outcomes, for example gender, age or ability. Then we can check whether the groups really are similar on all important variables.

Carry out the experiment meticulously

Once everything is in place, the experiment needs to be carried out. When carrying out the experiment, i.e. administering the pre-test, then carrying out the treatment and finally doing the post-test, we need to ensure that we control extraneous factors as much as possible. As we have seen above, if we wish to say something about what is cause (our treatment) and what is effect, we have to ensure that this control is maintained. This means two things: firstly, we will want to control the environment. It would be hard to conduct an experiment in an environment in which all kinds of other things are going on and be sure that whatever outcome we find is a result of the treatment (think of a classroom, for example). This is why many experiments are carried out in a laboratory where the researcher has complete control over the environment.

A second factor that we need to control is how the experiment is carried out. Every time we give the treatment to a subject, we must ensure that this is done in the same way. We need to do this to make sure that we do not introduce *experimenter bias*, the effect of the experimenter on the experiment. For example, if one experimenter giving our reading programme to students was really enthusiastic about the programme while another was very sceptical and communicated this to the students by saying things like, 'well, I'm not sure this will help you, it's only an experiment', we might well find different effects between the two.

Analyse the data

Once the experiment has been done and the post-test administered, we have to analyse the results. Typically, methods such as t-tests and analysis of variance are used. We will discuss these methods in Chapters 7 and 10 respectively. The results will then tell us whether we can provisionally reject our null hypothesis (the one we don't want to be true) or not.

■ ■ ■ Advantages and disadvantages of experimental research in education

Advantages

The main advantage of experimental research is the control over external factors mentioned several times in the previous section. Why do we want to control external factors and variables out of our experimental designs? We do this because it allows us to make a stronger claim to have determined *causality* than any other type of research.

One of the things we are often trying to do in quantitative research is determine what causes what – what is cause and what is effect. Often when talking about the results of research, the term 'cause' is used both frequently and loosely, e.g. 'an overly academic curriculum is a cause of pupil disaffection'. Many studies want to determine causes, and policy frequently wants to address causes of perceived problems (e.g. 'the causes of crime').

In fact causality is very hard to determine. Three main elements need to be present before we can say that one variable causes another:

1. There needs to be a *relationship* between the two variables. This relationship can be positive or negative. In a positive relationship, higher values on one variable will go together with higher values on another variable. For example, higher levels of achievement in school tend to be associated with higher levels of satisfaction with school. In a negative relationship lower values on one variable will be associated with higher variables on another. For example, in schools higher percentages of pupils with parents from low socio-economic status backgrounds will tend to be associated with lower levels of achievement on standardised tests. If there is no relationship, there is no causality. A variety of statistical methods exist to determine whether or not two or more variables are related, and I will discuss these in the following chapters.

2. There needs to be a *time order* between the two variables. In order to be able to say that a variable causes another, it must come before the other in time. Let's look at the relationship between birth order and achievement at school, for example. Some studies have found that there is a relationship between birth order and achievement in school (Muijs, 1997), with firstborns scoring higher than those born later. There is possibly a causal effect here. It would clearly be nonsense to hypothesise that school achievement causes birth order, as achievement follows birth order in time. In this case the direction of causality is clear: birth order would have to be cause and achievement effect. However, in many cases in educational research, things are not quite that clear-cut. Think, for example, about the relationship between a pupil's self-esteem and their achievement. Here it is not clear which comes first in time. Do pupils with lower self-esteem start doing worse because of this? Or does low achievement affect pupils' self-esteem negatively? Possibly the relationship is *reciprocal*, with both elements influencing one another in a circular relationship, lower achievement leading to lower self-esteem which in turn affects achievement. But which came first? This is often a chicken-and-egg type question that is extremely hard to solve.

3. The relationship found must not be the result of *confounding variables*. This means that the relationship cannot be explained by a third variable. A well-known example of this is the relationship between storks and births: in some European countries, the traditional answer when children ask their parents where babies come from is to say that storks bring them. Some statisticians have found strong evidence that this claim is in fact true: for example, Lowry (2002) reports that if one examines the records of the city of Copenhagen for the ten or twelve years following the Second World War there is a strong positive correlation between the number of storks nesting in the city annually and the number of human babies born in the city annually. Therefore storks bring babies – or do they? There is, in fact, a confounding variable here. During the ten or twelve years following the Second World War the population of Copenhagen (like that of most European cities) grew. As a result of this, there were more people of child-bearing age, and therefore more babies were born. Also as the population increased there was an increase in construction to accommodate this growth, which in turn provided more nesting places for storks which led to increasing numbers of storks being present in the city.

All three of these factors (a relationship, a time sequence and no confounding variable) need to be present before we can conclude that one variable causes another.

Why is experimental research better at determining causality than any other type of research? This follows from the element of control mentioned earlier. Factor one, establishing whether there is a relationship, can be done through any type of quantitative research and experiments are not necessarily better than non-experimental research at establishing this. However, the situation is different for the other two prerequisites for establishing a causal relationship. In experimental studies the researcher is manipulating the treatment so we can be certain of the time sequence. Likewise, the problem of extraneous variables causing a relationship is less strong in experimental research than in any other type of research because the experimenter can control the environment and ensure that as few extraneous factors are involved as possible, as we saw in the section on how to design experiments.

Does this mean that when we do an experiment and find a significant result, we can be certain of cause and effect? This is clearly not the case, for the following reasons:

1. Results from a single experiment may be due to chance. Only if research is *replicated*, i.e. the findings are repeated in different studies using different participants, preferably in slightly different settings, can we be certain of this.

2. It is always possible that findings are caused by an extraneous factor that we haven't thought of when setting up our experiment.

3. We are creating an artificial situation. Therefore the question remains: do these effects occur in real-life situations?

Disadvantages

This leads us to some of the weaknesses of the experimental approach. The laboratory set-up is always an artificial one, and the correspondence to real-life situations can be questionable. How applicable are the results of experiments to real-life educational situations? Here, the control that is an advantage of the experimental method becomes a disadvantage. In everyday settings, any causal effect found in an experimental setting is likely to be influenced by a whole load of contextual factors and influences which will tend to make the relationship far less predictable than in a laboratory setting. Remember, for example, the study on the effect of violent video games given in Example 2.1. While in an experimental study we may find an effect of watching these videos on children's behaviour, it is rare that children will be in a situation in which the video will be the *only* influence on their behaviour. When they are actually playing at school, for example, interactions with peers, school rules, weather, etc. will all influence their behaviour as well. If we look at the other example about presentation of material in animated form, we would have to question whether this effect really matters in practice, or if it is so small that it makes no real difference to learning in classroom situations compared to other factors (such as teacher interactions). Transferability is clearly an issue in educational experimental research.

Another problem with experimental research is that it can be difficult to put into practice in educational settings. Consider, for example, the issue of evaluating educational programmes and initiatives. We might want to do this using an experimental design because we want to see whether the intervention has caused an improvement in the school. We might want to develop an intervention to improve the reading performance of pupils and test whether this intervention is successful. A pure experimental design would involve randomly assigning pupils to the treatment and control groups in the school in which the experiment is taking place. This is often problematic in practice. Teachers and parents will be unlikely to be overly keen on this type of design, and there are obvious ethical issues in allowing one group of pupils to receive an intervention that we think/hope is effective while other pupils do not receive this intervention. In practical terms, realigning timetables etc. to facilitate the experimental design is also difficult. The difficulties are even larger when one is doing an experiment in a number of schools.

A further problem occurs when we are implementing an intervention that is specifically designed to take place in a classroom, such as a new teaching method. Obviously, there would be problems in trying to randomly allocate pupils to teachers who did and did not implement the intervention. As in the example above, this would be disruptive to the school, and lead to possible ethical issues as well as potentially to complaints from parents. Another major problem would be the lack of control over the environment. In a classroom situation, there is a whole variety of other influences that may affect outcomes, making it difficult to ascribe effects to the intervention. The teachers may be differentially effective, peers may influence each other, and so on. However, taking the intervention out of the classroom and putting it in the laboratory might make the results suspect with regards to transferability. If an intervention is supposed to work in the classroom, testing it in an artificial laboratory environment often would not seem sensible.

Because of these problems, educational interventions in schools are typically evaluated using *quasi-experimental designs*.

▓ ▓ ▓ Quasi-experimental designs

Quasi-experimental designs are meant to approximate as closely as possible the advantages of true experimental designs where the problems mentioned above occur, such as having to implement a programme in a natural school setting.

The main distinction between experimental and quasi-experimental research lies in the allocation of persons to groups. As we saw above, in traditional experimental research persons are allocated to groups through randomisation to minimise bias. Quasi-experiments are often used precisely because such random allocation is not possible or practical. Typically, the experimental group will be decided by which settings (e.g. schools, classrooms, factories) have volunteered or been selected to be part of the intervention. Therefore, rather than randomly allocating, we will have to choose a control group that is as similar to the experimental group as possible. Because we are not using random allocation, we call this control group the *comparison group* as it is not a pure control group. In order to retain the advantages of experimental designs (control over the environment) as much as possible, it is crucial to ensure that the experimental and comparison groups are as similar as possible. This is not an easy thing to do, because the number of variables that may affect outcomes in educational settings is substantial. Therefore the best we can do is think carefully about what factors can affect our outcomes and try to match the settings with these factors as far as we can.

■ ■ ■ Example 2.3

Evaluation of a professional development programme

Quasi-experimental research is especially suited to looking at the effects of an educational intervention, such as a school improvement programme, a project to improve a specific element (such as an anti-bullying programme) or a professional development programme.

In one example, Veenman et al. (1996) report on the evaluation of a Dutch initiative designed to improve teaching in secondary schools. Based on cognitive science and teacher effectiveness research, a programme of professional development was instigated to instruct teachers on using two direct instruction models, one directed at using well-structured skills, the other at developing higher-order thinking skills.

As part of their evaluation 27 teachers from three training colleges who had been trained in the model were compared with 24 teachers from parallel classes in the same teacher training colleges who had not been trained in the model, in order to look at whether or not the student teachers had implemented these strategies. All teachers were observed by trained observers prior to and following the intervention, and the performance of these trainee teachers was rated by the observers at

▶

both time points using a specially developed behaviour rating scale (see next chapter for more on designing observation scales). The treatment and comparison groups did not differ significantly in the pre-test observations on any factor, except on task behaviour which was 84 per cent in the treatment and 77 per cent in the control group. This was therefore factored into the analyses of variance used to interrogate the post-test data (see Chapter 10 for an explanation of this statistical method). Following the intervention (training in the direct instruction models for the experimental group, regular instruction in the comparison group), the trainee teachers were again observed using the rating scale. It was found that the experimental group teachers outperformed the comparison group teachers on all subscales of the rating scale.

This is a good example of the use of quasi-experimental methodology to look at the effects of an intervention, which in this case was aimed at improving the effectiveness of student teachers. Using parallel classes as the comparison group should ensure that the groups are comparable, as students are usually assigned to classes in a random manner. The same observation scale was used in both groups, ensuring comparability, and observers were thoroughly trained. What was not clear from this article is whether or not observers were aware which was the experimental and which the comparison group. If they were aware of this, there is the possibility that bias may creep in because of it (i.e. observers may be inclined to rate teachers in the experimental group more positively).

Pupil background factors represent one element that is important to most educational outcomes, whether it be attitudes to school, well-being or achievement. The comparison and experimental groups must be as similar as possible in terms of factors such as parental socio-economic status, gender, ethnicity and ability. In a within-school design, for example, one would not be able to implement a programme in a low set class, compare it to a high set and then conclude that any differences were due to the intervention rather than differences between the pupils in ability. Likewise, comparing a school in a deprived area with one in a leafy suburb would make it impossible to say that any effect found was due to the programme rather than differences in pupils' socio-economic background. Therefore, we need to try to match comparison schools, classrooms, etc. as closely as possible to those in the experimental group on these factors.

However, pupil background is by no means the only set of variables that may differ between experimental and comparison groups and that may affect outcomes. Teacher quality has been found to be a major factor affecting pupil achievement, as have factors such as school leadership, school climate and peer group effects. Also, it is important to remember that there are usually other interventions going on in a school at the same time as the one you are studying. For example, as well as a reading intervention that is being evaluated, a school may be putting in place a state-mandated literacy strategy.

While it would be good practice to match comparison to experimental groups on all these factors where possible, this is usually very difficult to achieve. As a researcher you will have to try and collect as much information as possible on as many variables as you think might be relevant to outcomes when doing quasi-experimental research. One can then try and statistically control for the effects of these variables.

Obviously, from the point of view of establishing causality, this is not as effective a method as using a pure experimental design. It is clear from the above that finding a comparison group that is exactly matched to the experimental group is an especially difficult task and that the lack of randomisation will lead to the possibility of bias creeping in. Even if we have managed to match our experimental and comparison groups on all variables we can think of, there may be additional factors specific to the culture of the setting (school or classroom) that may be affecting results. Nonetheless, by using a matched experimental–comparison design, we are better able to see whether our intervention has been successful or not than in any other way save for a real experiment. This is because we are still controlling as many factors as we can and as far as possible comparing like with like (experimental and control group), which we would not be doing if we used a survey approach, for example (see Chapter 3).

Quasi-experimental research designs do have one clear advantage over pure experimental designs, which is that they are studied in natural educational settings. If we find programme effects we can at least be confident that these work in real schools and classrooms with all their complexity rather than just in the laboratory setting. This makes quasi-experimental research a good way of evaluating new initiatives and programmes in education.

The basic structure of a quasi-experimental study is pretty much the same as that of an experimental study. As in an experimental study, we start with research objectives and hypotheses (e.g. our intervention will lead to higher performance in reading) and then design the quasi-experiment. The design in question will not be dissimilar to an experimental design, with a pre-test, followed by the intervention, followed by a post-test of both the experimental and the comparison group. As in experimental designs, it is possible to have several variations of the treatment or intervention and to have more than one experimental group, and it might be necessary to provide some sort of placebo. However, in the present educational climate multiple initiatives are likely to be under way in any one school, so a school 'where nothing is going on' is unlikely to be found and we may not need a placebo in all cases.

Selecting appropriate instruments to test our hypotheses is just as important here as in experimental designs (or, as we will see, in survey designs), and we need to ensure that if we are using a test or a questionnaire it is administered in similar conditions in both the experimental and comparison schools, preferably in the presence of the researcher. Otherwise test-taking conditions could affect outcomes. Whatever outcome measure we use it must be the same in the experimental and comparison schools, otherwise we are not comparing like with like.

Once matched comparison and experimental settings have been selected we need to pre-test in all settings. In a pure experiment, we would then 'carry out the experiment meticulously'. In real-life settings this aspect of meticulous control of the intervention is neither possible nor desirable in every case. When implementing educational interventions it has been found that taking account of the specific context of the school, classroom or faculty where it is being implemented is likely to enhance the effectiveness of the intervention (Harris, 2001). As programme developers we would therefore not necessarily not want to specify that the intervention be carried out in exactly the same way in all settings. What we will need to do instead is monitor closely exactly how the intervention is being implemented in different settings, and what the content elements of the intervention are. To do this we might need to use alternative methods, such as surveys, observation and qualitative methods. This should allow us to map what elements have been more and less successful.

■ ■ ■ Common misconceptions

1. *If I find that something works in an experiment, I know it will work in the classroom.* While experiments are the best way to determine cause and effect, the artificial conditions under which they occur make it hard to say whether or not the results will easily translate to the complex reality of educational settings. This needs to be empirically tested.

2. *But if I find that something works in an experiment, I can be sure of cause and effect, right?* Well, more sure than by using any other method. However, there may be an underlying cause or confounding factor we haven't thought of, or we may be finding an effect by coincidence. Therefore only replication of findings can make us certain that what we are finding is true causality.

3. *Experimental methods are the only truly scientific research method.* This misconception, common among some policy-makers, comes from the fact that experimental methods are widely used in the 'hard' sciences (e.g. physics, chemistry) and that they are ideally suited to solving cause-and-effect style problems. However, as we have seen above, experiments are not necessarily best suited to looking at issues as they occur in real-life educational settings which are complex and multifaceted. Scientific educational research is about solving problems or answering questions in a rigorous manner. There are many different questions that we can ask, and many different methods that we can use to try and answer these questions rigorously, including non-experimental quantitative research and qualitative methods such as case studies, ethnography and interviews.

4. *A quasi-experiment is pretty much the same as an experiment, isn't it.* Yes, but there are a number of important differences. Firstly, as we are not assigning persons to groups randomly, we cannot be certain that we are controlling for relevant differences between the groups. That makes inferences about causality more uncertain. Also, because the intervention takes place in a real-life setting, we cannot be sure that implementation is identical. Often this isn't even desirable. Both of these mean that we need to collect more data than in real experimental studies to make sure that we can come to reasonably clear conclusions.

■ ■ ■ Summary

In experimental designs we typically compare two or more groups, one of which (the experimental group) receives the experimental treatment, while the other (the control group) does not. Experimental studies usually employ a pre-test–experiment–post test design. Subjects are randomly assigned to groups, ensuring minimal bias. Both groups are pre-tested using a suitable outcome measure. Then the treatment is administered meticulously, and a post-test conducted. We can then look at whether or not the outcomes differ between the experimental and control group.

Experimental research is the best method for examining causal relationships because the method allows us to look at the three main questions that need to be answered in the affirmative before we can say that one variable causes another: is there a relationship between the variables, does our cause precede our effect in time, and are there any confounding variables that could explain the relationship? A problem with experiments is that they take place in artificial environments (the laboratory) that are quite different from typically complex and multifaceted educational settings. This means that we can't be certain that findings from experiments will necessary hold in real-life settings. Experiments can also be difficult to implement in education.

This means that we often have to go with the 'second best option' in terms of determining causality, quasi-experiments. In quasi-experiments, rather than randomly assigning persons to the experimental and control groups, we will try to match the experimental group (typically a class or school in which an intervention is taking place) with a comparison group. We will have to try to make the comparison group as similar to the experimental group as possible on all factors except for the treatment, although it will not usually be possible to get complete parity. Other than that, the basic pre-test post-test design will be similar to that used in pure experimental research. Because we are not randomly allocating, we need to collect as much data as possible on those variables where treatment and comparison group may differ and that could affect the outcomes.

■ ■ ■ Exercises

1. What are the main differences between experimental and quasi-experimental studies?

2. 'Correlation does not imply causality.' Do you agree with this statement? Why? Why not?

3. If experiments are the best way of determining causality, why would we want to do any other kind of research?

4. I want to know whether my school improvement project is improving pupils' attitudes to school. Can you design a study that looks at this?

5. I have noticed that my pupils seem to be hyperactive when they have drunk soft drinks during break time. I want to know whether consuming soft drinks leads to lower concentration levels in pupils immediately following consumption. Can you design a study that looks at this?

6. I want to know whether teacher motivation improves pupil performance or whether it is higher pupil performance that motivates teachers. Is it possible to determine this? If yes, how would you do that?

■ ■ ■ Further reading

A key text is Campbell, D. T. and Stanley, J. C. (1966) *Experimental and Quasi-Experimental Designs for Research* (Houghton-Mifflin). Although an older work, this is the classic reference book on experimental and quasi-experimental designs and is still unsurpassed in the field. However, it is quite heavy reading.

Another classic work on the subject that has been recently updated is Shadish, W. R. and Cook, T. D. (2001) *Experimental and Quasi-Experimental Designs for Generalised Causal Inference* (Houghton-Mifflin).

A user-friendly but comprehensive introduction written for psychologists is Christensen, L. (2000) *Experimental Methodology* (Allyn & Bacon). Other types of quantitative research are also briefly discussed.

The classic reference book on quasi-experimental designs is Cook, T. D. and Campbell, D. T. (1979) *Quasi Experimentation* (Houghton-Mifflin).

■ ■ ■ Chapter 3

Designing non-experimental studies

In contrast to experimental research, which is a clearly defined research method, non-experimental quantitative research is more varied. Non-experimental methods include survey research, historical research, observation and analysis of existing data sets. In this chapter we will discuss the most common methods in educational research: survey research, observational research and analysing existing data sets.

■ ■ ■ Survey research

Probably the most popular (quantitative) research design in the social sciences is survey research. Survey research designs are quite flexible and can therefore appear in a variety of forms, but all are characterised by the collection of data using standard questionnaire forms administered by telephone or face to face, by postal pencil-and-paper questionnaires or increasingly by using web-based and e-mail forms.

All of us are likely to have had some experience of survey research, if not as developers then as participants in one of the many surveys carried out on our consumption patterns. This ubiquity makes many feel that survey research is the easiest form of research which can be done in a 'quick and dirty' way. Many organisations design in-house surveys to look at a variety of questions. However, as we will see below, designing survey research is not that simple. There is a variety of pitfalls and dangers, and many studies manage to fall into pretty much all of them.

■ ■ ■ **Example 3.1**

The relationship between school factors and pupils' well-being

There are many examples of survey studies in educational research.

In one study, Opdenakker and Van Damme (2000) looked at the effects of school factors on pupils' well-being in Flemish secondary schools. The authors used a sample of 4,889 pupils in the first year of secondary school (pupils were in 276 classes in 52 schools). Social and affective outcomes were the dependent variable. These were measured using a pupil questionnaire designed to measure eight factors of pupil well-being. Pupils were given a number of ability tests and a questionnaire measuring their achievement motivation. School factors were measured by a questionnaire given to a random sample of 15 teachers in each school, designed to tap their teaching practice and school life. The variables were reduced to six main factors: teaching staff cooperation in relation to teaching methods, focus on discipline and subject matter, attention to pupil differences and development, orderly learning environment, cooperation and cohesion among school staff, traditional style of teaching, cultural education and creativity, and focus on educational and personal development. Teaching staff cooperation in relation to teaching methods was positively related to pupil well-being. Creating an orderly learning environment and a traditional style of teaching had a positive effect on pupils with a high learning motivation and a negative effect on pupils with low learning motivation. The other factors were not related to pupil well-being.

This study is a good example of the use of survey research in education, although some of the 'causal' language ('has an effect on') is hard to demonstrate in a survey study.

Designing a survey study

The phases in designing a survey study are similar to those in experimental research. The differences lie in how we design the study, design the instruments and collect the data.

Define research objectives

As with experimental research we start by defining our research objectives. A wide variety of research questions can be studied using survey methods. If our main interest is causality, we may want to look at whether it is possible to use experimental or quasi-experimental methods. Survey research is well suited to descriptive studies, or where researchers want to look at relationships between variables occurring in particular real-life contexts.

Research designs should be realistic and feasible. In survey research in particular, the temptation is to specify a very extensive research design which attempts to capture the full complexity of the world. Often, it will not be possible to collect data on all the variables we might want to include because of financial and time constraints, and we may have to settle for a sample that is a bit smaller than we would have liked. Where this is the case, the key is to select those variables that we think are most likely to affect our outcomes.

Once we have defined our research objectives, we can proceed to the research design which will be dependent on those objectives. For example, if we wanted to look at how teachers' views of effective pedagogy changed over time we would have to do a *longitudinal* study, surveying the teachers over a number of years. If we wanted to find out about teachers' opinions on a new policy initiative by the department for education, a *cross-sectional study* where you would just survey teachers once, would suffice. If we wanted to survey whether teachers' opinions had changed following an intervention, pre- and post-surveys would be suitable. We might also want to mix different methods, for example a large-scale survey followed by in-depth interviews of a small subsample. A range of options are possible, depending on research objectives and, not least, research budgets. The latter are an important constraint in educational research (and social scientific research more generally) and have led to a situation in which most studies are one-off cross-sectional designs. This is unfortunate, as many research questions would benefit from a more longitudinal approach.

Formulate hypotheses

While in experimental designs it is common to develop and test hypotheses in all cases, this is not necessarily so in survey designs. Often, we will want to make specific predictions about relationships between variables in the form of hypotheses (e.g. 'there is a relationship between self-concept and achievement'). Generally speaking, the flexibility of survey research means that these can be more wide-ranging and complex than in experimental studies (e.g. 'the relationship between self-concept and achievement will increase as the child gets older'; 'the relationship between self-concept and achievement will be mediated by emotional intelligence'). However, not all survey studies test specific hypotheses. Some survey studies can be purely descriptive. For example, one common use of survey studies is to look at voting intentions. Researchers do not start from specific hypotheses (e.g. 'the Democratic share of the vote is hypothesised to be more than 40 per cent'), but merely wish to test what voters' intentions are. Therefore, whether one wants to test specific hypotheses or conduct a more descriptive study (e.g. 'what percentage of teachers has engaged in professional development activities over the past year?') will depend on your research question.

Define what information you need

Once research questions and, where necessary, hypotheses have been decided on, you need to think about what information is needed to answer these research questions. If your research objectives suggest that a survey study would be a suitable method, you need to decide what information you will need to collect through your survey study. This will involve deciding what questions to ask, whether to use pre-published scales, how long to make your survey and so on. We will look at a number of these later on in this chapter.

Decide what your population is

As well as deciding on what information you need, you also need to decide exactly what your *population* is going to be. The population is the group you want to generalise your findings to. For example, you might want to do a study on the relationship between self-concept and achievement. Your population could be all 10-year-olds in the county, all 10-year-olds in the country and so on. It is important to be clear what your population is, as this will determine who you are (in most cases) going to *sample*. Of course, in some cases it may not be necessary to sample at all. It may be possible to survey the whole population. If, for example, I wanted to do a survey of my students' views of my teaching in the undergraduate statistics class, I could give a questionnaire to the whole population, as the population size is quite small (14 students this year). Sampling the whole population is known as a *census*. It is also possible to (attempt to) sample even a large population given enough resources. Governments, for example, regularly conduct a census of their population, although, as recent examples in the United States and the United Kingdom have shown, this process is not without problems and not all members of the population are actually reached. In most cases, we do not have the resources to study the whole population and will need to sample. It is important to remember that we can only generalise to a population we have actually sampled from. And therefore some thought about exactly what our population is going to be is warranted.

Decide how to sample from the population

In most cases we will need to take a sample from our population. We will then usually want to generalise the results we find in our sample to our population. After all, a survey of the voting intentions of a sample of 1,000 people would not be very useful if we couldn't generalise our findings from that sample to voters as a whole! In order for us to be able to generalise, we need to have an *unbiased* sample of the population, which means that we want our sample to be representative of the population we are studying, and not skewed towards one group or another. If we were trying to generalise to all 10-year-olds, for example, we wouldn't want to sample only all-girls schools. The best way of ensuring that our sample is unbiased is by using *probability sampling methods*.

The most well-known of these is *simple random sampling*. In a typical simple random sample everyone in the population has exactly the same chance of being included in the sample. This is because the sample is drawn at random from the population (for example, by putting names in a hat or, more typically nowadays, by using random number generators). That makes it the most unbiased form of sampling, and this is the method used to draw lottery numbers, for example. Saying that this is the most unbiased sampling method would suggest that it is a good idea to attempt to use simple random sampling at all times. However, when one looks at actual educational research, it is clear that the majority of studies do not in fact use this method. Why is this? There are a number of reasons, some good, some less so.

One good reason is that while simple random samples are excellent for generalising to the population as a whole, we might in some cases want to generalise to a specific subpopulation that is too small to be reliably picked up in any but the largest of samples. We might, for example, want to compare the well-being of students in private and state-run schools. Taking a random sample of 1,000 pupils may leave us with only a very small group of students in private schools. Therefore, to ensure a suitably large number in both, we might want to use *stratified random sampling.* Doing this involves first dividing the population into the groups we want to study, in this case private and state-school attendees, and then randomly sampling from each group separately, so we would obtain a sample of 500 pupils in private and 500 in state-run schools.

Sometimes, we may want to ensure that different subgroups are represented in our sample in accordance with their presence in the population. Again, unless you take a very large sample, this will be difficult to achieve for small subgroups. Therefore, we sometimes specify in advance what proportion of those groups we want to have in our sample and sample until that quota is fulfilled. For example, we may have a population in which 10 per cent of pupils are of Afro-Caribbean descent. In *quota sampling*, as this method is called, we will sample Afro-Caribbeans until we have reached our quota, in this case 10 per cent of 1,000, or 100 Afro-Caribbeans.

Another reason not to use simple random sampling lies in the problem of being able to draw conclusions about sites in which members of the population are nested. For example, in educational research we are often interested in things happening in schools, or school effects, and how these may influence students in those schools. Saying anything about school (or classroom teaching) effects would be difficult if we used simple random sampling. Even if we were to have a large sample of 100 students, it is likely that they would be spread over a very large number of schools, meaning that in most cases we would have one pupil or maybe two in any given school. Obviously, it would be nonsensical to extrapolate effects of the school or teacher from findings on one pupil in that school! Therefore, when we want to look at school effects we will usually sample schools randomly, and then survey all pupils in that school. More generally, using *cluster sampling* we will randomly sample higher-level sites in which members of the population are clustered, and then survey all respondents in those sites. A related method is *multistage sampling* in which we first sample higher-level sites (e.g. local education authorities) at random, then randomly sample a lower stage (e.g. schools in those LEAs), and then randomly sample members of the population in that stage (e.g. pupils within a school). This can be done for any number of stages, the three given here being just an example, and is often used in electoral studies.

A problem with cluster and multistage sampling methods is that they are no longer purely random. This is because generally speaking people who are clustered within a site (e.g. pupils in a school) are more similar than they are across sites. If we think about schools, we know that within schools pupils are likely to be more homogeneous with respect to social background (due to catchment area effects) than the population of pupils as a whole. Also, the very fact of being within a site, e.g. a school, will tend to make people more similar, as they are subject to the same peer group effects and culture of the organisation. This leads to problems when we are doing statistical analyses in that we will need to use methods that have been designed specially for this type of sample, as we will see in Chapter 11.

The above are all probability sampling methods, and if used properly we can be reasonably confident that we have an unbiased approximation of the population. However, probability sampling methods are not necessarily the most common sampling methods in educational research. Two other sampling methods appear to be particularly frequent. One popular method is *volunteer sampling*. Volunteer sampling occurs when we ask people to volunteer to take part in our research, through an advertisement in a local paper or professional publication, a notice on a university campus, etc. This method has the obvious advantage of being easy and cheap but is highly problematic from the point of view of obtaining an unbiased sample. People who volunteer to take part in survey research are often untypical. They are likely to be those people who have particularly strong views on the research subject or have a lot of time on their hands. Often, volunteering is encouraged by giving a (financial) reward to participants. This can help alleviate bias to some extent, but unless the reward is substantial this is unlikely to attract respondents who enjoy a good income. Bias is therefore a serious problem with this sampling method.

Probably the most common sampling method in educational studies at present is *convenience sampling*. This occurs where researchers have easy access to particular sites, such as teachers they have worked with before or pupils in their own schools, and use those people in their research. This method has obvious advantages in terms of cost and convenience but suffers from serious problems of bias, as the sites they have easy access to may not be representative of the population. For example, if the researcher works in a rural school, the pupils will differ in many respects from those in an inner-city environment. This limits the generalisability of results to those areas that are similar, remembering that geographic area may also be a factor that differentiates pupils. Therefore, wherever possible, it is advisable to use probability sampling methods.

Design your research instruments

The next stage of survey research is to design the survey instruments, for example a written questionnaire, a phone questionnaire or an online survey questionnaire. As mentioned in Chapter 2 on experimental research, this is a crucially important process because once the data are collected we will not be able to rectify any problems with the instruments. It is clear that the quality of the data will depend on the quality of the instruments, and we will further discuss issues regarding the design of survey instruments below.

Collect the data

Data collection is the next phase, and another one where problems can occur in survey studies. Data can be collected through pencil-and-paper questionnaires, telephone or face-to-face interviews and online methods such as web-based questionnaires (see box).

■ ■ ■ Advantages and disadvantages of different data collection methods

There are a number of different ways to conduct a survey, each with their advantages and disadvantages.

■ Probably the most common method in educational research is the use of the *pencil-and-paper questionnaire*. The main advantage of this method is its familiarity to users, the fact that it allows users to complete the questionnaire at their own convenience, and the fact that it allows them some time to think about their answers. Disadvantages are often low response rates (see text), and time-consuming follow-up and data entry.

■ *Telephone interviews* allow the interviewer to continue until the target sample size is met and are better suited to quota sampling methods than paper-and-pencil questionnaires. They often allow for direct

▶

input of answers into a computer system, saving valuable data input time. It is also easy to make these questionnaires adaptive, in that one can vary questions based on previous responses. However, bias can occur in telephone interviews. While in western countries most people are connected to the telephone system, some are not listed in telephone directories. Also, many find telephone questionnaires intrusive and will refuse to participate. There is little time for respondents to think over answers. When doing telephone interviews, it is important to ensure that phone calls are made at a time when respondents are available.

■ *Face-to-face interviews* again allow the interviewer to reach sample size targets and quotas and can be adaptive, but like phone interviews can be seen as intrusive and therefore induce non-cooperation. The place that is chosen to conduct face-to-face interviews can introduce bias, as in the practice of interviewing in shopping malls during daytime, where one is unlikely to reach those who are working during that time. Face-to-face interviews wil involve as much data input as pencil-and-paper questionnaires.

■ We are currently seeing a strong growth in *online and e-mail questionnaires*. In essence, these are similar to pencil-and-paper questionnaires, with the advantage that answers can be directly stored in a database or even directly analysed, saving data input time and costs. Like telephone and face-to-face questionnaires they can be made adaptive. However, a major disadvantage of online questionnaires at present is that penetration is still relatively low, and you therefore need to consider carefully if you can fully reach the population you want to study using this method, and not just a subset that is younger and more wealthy than average. Technophobia can also be a problem in some populations.

Whatever sampling method we use, we will have to confront the problem of non-response to the survey. In pencil-and-paper questionnaires this takes the form of non-returned questionnaires. The number of unreturned questionnaires can often be very substantial with many questionnaires receiving response rates well below 50 per cent, and virtually none (save small-scale questionnaires completed involuntarily, such as compulsory student feedback) receiving a 100 per cent response rate. This non-response wouldn't matter if we could be certain that those that do not respond are very similar to respondents on all relevant variables and therefore would have answered the survey similarly if they had taken part. However, this is by no means certain, and in many cases we can be sure that this is not the case. Generally, people who feel more strongly or have a particular axe to grind about the subject are more likely to respond, as are people with an interest in research more generally. Also, people with more time on their hands tend to respond more readily to questionnaires.

Low response rates obviously make our final sample smaller, which means we have less 'statistical power' to test our hypotheses. Therefore, we need to try and maximise our response rates. There are a number of things we can do to help:

1. Keep the questionnaire sufficiently short (30 minutes maximum) and attractive.
2. Provide pre-paid addressed envelopes to minimise cost and effort to respondents.
3. Promise (and provide!) respondents who complete and return the questionnaire feedback on the research project.
4. Provide a reward for completion. Book tokens, vouchers, etc. are usually suitable (this is an expensive option, though).
5. Follow-up phone calls and visits to participants may help improve response rates quite considerably.
6. Allow respondents to complete the questionnaire either through the mail, on the web or by e-mail.
7. A final factor that affects response rates is credibility of the person or organisation conducting the study. Institutions of higher education and government bodies tend to have higher credibility among respondents than commercial organisations and therefore get higher response rates. Also, having an established relationship with the respondents will help improve response rates.

Non-response takes on slightly different forms in telephone and face-to-face formats, in that it is always possible to continue phoning/interviewing until a certain target response number has been reached. However, this does not solve the problem of non-participants (those people that have refused to take part) being in some way different from those that have agreed to participate, and the same issues as with survey research remain. Therefore it is again best to try and maximise initial response rates and minimise the number of non-respondents. The methods we can use to help us achieve this are similar to those mentioned with respect to pencil-and-paper questionnaires:

1. Keep the questionnaire sufficiently short.
2. Phone or contact people at a time convenient to them and arrange another date or time for the interview if necessary.
3. Promise and provide respondents with feedback on the research project.
4. Provide a reward for completion.
5. Follow up visits and phone calls.
6. Again, credibility is a factor.

None of these methods will totally eradicate non-response, and we therefore need to carefully consider what factors can lead to non-response and how we can correct for differences between non-respondents and respondents.

Analyse the data

The final step is data analysis. We can use a large variety of methods when analysing survey data. These will be discussed in the following chapters.

Advantages and disadvantages of survey research

Survey research has a number of advantages that have made it the most popular type of research in social sciences. First of all, survey research is highly flexible. It is possible to study a wide range of research questions using survey methods. You can describe a situation, study relationships between variables and so on. Because survey research does not set up an artificial situation like an experiment, it is easier to generalise findings to real-world settings, as this is where the research takes place. Survey studies are also efficient in terms of our being able to gather large amounts of data at reasonably low cost and effort compared to other methods like observation. It is also easy to guarantee respondents' anonymity, especially with pencil-and-paper, Internet and telephone questionnaires, which may lead to more candid answers than less anonymous methods like interviews. Survey research is therefore particularly suited for canvassing opinions and feelings about particular issues. The use of standardised questions allows for easy comparability between respondents and groups of respondents (differences between men and women, for example).

Obviously, surveys do not allow the researcher to control the environment and are therefore less suited to answering questions of causality than experimental designs. Nevertheless, by collecting data on as many relevant variables as possible, using longitudinal designs and careful statistical modelling it is sometimes possible to tentatively reach a view on cause and effect, although it will never be as clear-cut as in an experiment. A further limitation is that it is difficult to come to deeper understanding of processes and contextual differences through questionnaires, which are standardised and by their nature limited in length and depth of responses. A combination of survey and qualitative methods can help here. Finally, while questionnaires are highly suited to gathering information on respondents' perceptions and opinions of a situation, gathering information on respondent behaviours can be problematic as self-reports are not always reliable in this respect (see Muijs, forthcoming). Some studies have, for example, found large differences between teachers' reports of their classroom practice and their actual classroom practice as observed by outsiders.

Designing survey questionnaires

It has been mentioned before that the way data is collected is crucial to the quality of the research undertaken. Therefore designing a questionnaire, whether it is to be administered by phone, pencil and paper or on the web, is a key part of survey research. Regrettably, too many researchers assume that this is an easy task and take little care when designing a questionnaire which is why there are many low-quality questionnaires about. The way questionnaires are designed and questions are worded will affect the answers respondents give. Therefore it is important to think carefully about what kind of questions you want to ask.

There are a number of question types we can include in a survey instrument. The first distinction to make is that between *open-ended* and *closed questions*. Open-ended questions allow the respondent to formulate their own answer, whereas closed questions make the respondent choose between answers provided by the researcher.

An example of an open-ended question is:

What teaching method do you think is best for teaching reading?

....

....

A closed question would be:

Which method do you think is best for teaching reading (choose one answer only)?

Analytic phonics

Systematic phonics

A balanced approach

A whole language approach

You will not be surprised to hear that both have advantages and disadvantages. Open-ended questions have the advantage of allowing the respondent to freely formulate an answer. This can be important, as it allows you as a researcher to discover opinions or answers that you had not thought about before. In closed questions answers are limited to those you have formulated at the start, with no room for surprises. Inclusion of an 'other' category will only remedy this to a limited extent, as the respondent will be influenced by the answers presented in the preceding categories and is less likely to choose this option. However, open-ended questions are more difficult and time-consuming to work with because the answers will first need to be coded and quantified using some form of content analysis. There is also a loss of standardisation and comparability of answers across respondents. Finally, open-ended questions are more time-consuming for respondents, who will as a result be more inclined not to answer this type of question than closed questions.

The category of closed questions is itself quite broad, encompassing a range of question types. A first type is the *yes/no* question (e.g. 'Do you agree with the government's policy on classroom assistants, yes or no'). This is obviously an easy form for respondents, but on the other hand it does not provide a lot of subtlety in responses. For example, you might, want to know to what extent respondents agree with government policies. In that case, it is better to use some form of *rating scale*. Rating scales allow the respondent to choose one of several options indicating level of agreement or opinion on an item. Rating scales can take on a number of forms, and can have a differing number of response categories. Examples are as follows:

Rating scale example 1

I think all teachers in the country should receive a £10,000 pay rise (please choose one answer).

Strongly agree   Agree   Disagree   Strongly disagree   Don't know

Rating scale example 2

I think all teachers in the country should receive a £10,000 pay rise (please choose one answer).

Agree   Neither agree nor disagree   Disagree   Don't know

Rating scale example 3

I think all teachers in the country should receive a £10,000 pay rise.
(Please rate your agreement on the ten-point scale, with 10 being agree strongly, and 0 being disagree strongly.)

Agree strongly 10 9 8 7 6 5 4 3 2 1 0   Disagree strongly

Rating scale example 4

I think all teachers in the country should receive a £10,000 pay rise.
(Please rate your agreement by putting a cross on the line at the position that best reflects your level of agreement with this statement.)

Agree strongly _____ Disagree strongly

The first two examples are traditional rating scales on which respondents can choose a specific answer from a number of categories, usually between three and seven. The reason for not usually including more than seven categories is that it becomes hard for the respondent to make such fine distinctions. Imagine, for example, a 9-point scale answer to the above question: agree strongly, agree quite strongly, agree, agree weakly, neither agree nor disagree and so on. It is clearly becoming harder to make some of these distinctions. Now think of adding another four categories. As you can see, this quickly becomes unmanageable.

A contested question is whether or not to include a middle, neutral category (neither true nor untrue). A reason for not doing so is that answers to this category are often difficult to interpret, as some respondents who do not understand the question or don't have an opinion choose this option. In that case, you are left to wonder what a response in this category means: an actual 'neither true nor untrue of me', a 'don't know', a 'don't understand the question'? This problem can be at least partly alleviated by including a 'don't know' category at the end of the scale (never in the middle, otherwise you will be causing the same confusion). Another problem can be that including the middle category can encourage respondents to 'sit on the fence', which some respondents do very frequently. This is called the *central tendency* problem and is most likely to occur with more sensitive or controversial questions. To avoid this, we can choose not to use a middle category. On the other hand, some respondents may be genuinely neutral and by not using a middle category we might be misrepresenting their views.

The problem with this type of rating scale is that it is *ordinal* (see Chapter 4), which means that we cannot say whether the mathematical distance between, say, agree and agree strongly is the same as between agree and disagree. This limits our statistical analysis possibilities, so many researchers have tried to come up with ways to develop scales that are *continuous*, akin to tape measures. Examples 3 and 4 are ways of trying to do that. Example 3 presents one solution, which is to give respondents the opportunity to mark out of ten so they will think of it as a continuous scale. Example 4 is more ambitious, attempting to get an accurate measurement by getting the respondents to indicate a point on the line which is then measured for each respondent as a distance from agree strongly. In theory, both methods should be better able to provide continuous scales, but it has been questioned whether respondents are actually making such subtle distinctions when answering the question. This is especially true for example 4, which in theory is a perfectly continuous scale but in practice may be influenced by vagaries of marking by respondents.

A problem that can occur in questionnaires is that of *positive response bias*. This mainly occurs if respondents are asked about their views on a number of desirable or popular alternatives. Respondents may rate all of these equally favourably, making it difficult to see which option they would really prefer. Take, for example, the following possible goals of education:

- academic achievement
- a caring environment
- developing positive attitudes to learning
- a student-centred environment
- developing enterprising citizens
- enhancing pupils' self-esteem.

If we asked respondents (teachers in this case) to rate individual items using rating scales we are likely to find that all are rated highly by teachers. That would not give us a good indication of which element they really find the most important. To remedy this we would need to use some sort of forced choice format, by either asking them to rank the choices from 1 to 6 in order of importance (example 5 below) or by forcing them to choose between two options (example 6 below). If we use enough choices we can again calculate rankings.

Rating scale example 5

Please rank the following goals in order of importance for your school from first to sixth, with 1 indicating most important goal, 2 second most important goal and so on.

— High academic achievement

— A caring environment

— A student-centred environment

— Developing positive attitudes to learning

— Developing enterprising citizens

— Enhancing pupils' self-esteem

Rating scale example 6

Please indicate which of the following two goals you think is most important:

High academic achievement *OR* A caring environment

As well as issues to do with what type of question to use, there are a number of other factors to take into account when developing a questionnaire:

1. Keep it brief. The first element of good questionnaires, whatever way they are administered, is that they should not be too long. This is because lengthy questionnaires will annoy respondents, leading to higher levels of non-response or to respondents getting bored and not completing the questionnaire accurately. There is a slight conflict here with the imperative to try and collect as much data as possible, but it must be remembered that if the data you have collected is inaccurate, it doesn't help you to have a lot of it! Four sides of A4 is a good rule of thumb for maximum questionnaire length.

2. Keep your questions clear and simple. Ambiguously worded questions will lead to ambiguous responses, so it is important to phrase questions in such a way that they are understandable to all respondents. It is best to err on the side of caution here, and to remember that what may be clear to you as a researcher may not be clear to respondents. Use of acronyms is to be avoided, and where technical terms are used it is good practice to explain them.

3. Usually in a survey we will want to collect some data on respondent characteristics such as age, experience, gender and social background (e.g. occupation). Not all respondents enjoy answering this kind of question, and some will refuse to do so. It is therefore good practice to put this type of question at the end rather than, as is common, at the beginning of the questionnaire. This is because if you annoy respondents at the start, they are unlikely to complete your questionnaire.

4. Include a 'don't know' category in rating scales to give respondents who do not have an answer or an opinion a chance to make this choice. This is particularly important if you are using rating scales with a neutral mid-point, otherwise those respondents who wish to answer 'don't know' are likely to choose this mid-point, making their answer hard to interpret.

5. Double negatives ('if you don't disagree …') should always be avoided in questionnaires, as they lead to confusion among respondents who have to complete extra cognitive action to interpret the question.

6. Ask only one question in any item. This seems obvious but is in practice often forgotten. It is easy to succumb to the temptation of

putting two questions into one item, such as 'Do you think Reading Recovery is an effective and efficient way of improving reading scores of low achieving readers?' The issue here is that both the respondent and yourself will have problems interpreting this question and the answers. A respondent may think Reading Recovery is effective but not efficient in terms of cost or time. What does she answer? Likewise, when you receive responses to this question, how do you interpret them? Does a negative response mean the respondent thinks the programme is both ineffective and inefficient? Or just ineffective?

7. Take into account cultural differences. It is important to make sure your instruments are culturally sensitive. Avoid items or wordings that may be unclear or offensive to different cultures, such as asking respondents for their 'Christian name'.

The single most effective strategy to minimise problems is to make sure you *pilot* your instruments. Test them first by having colleagues read them. Following that, use them with a small group of people from the population you want to sample. Ask them to provide feedback on the instrument and test the instrument statistically to see if there are any unusual response patterns that could indicate that certain items have not been properly understood.

■ ■ ■ Observational research

Another research method that is used quite often in education is observational research. Observation in classrooms or nursery settings has been found to be a useful way of looking at many educational research questions, such as whether girls and boys play differently, or whether teacher behaviours influence student achievement.

Advantages and disadvantages of observational research

Observational studies have a number of advantages compared to survey research. The main ones are as follows:

■ Observational research can give direct access to social interactions. This is advantageous when we want to find out what actually happens in a setting rather than what is reported to us by participants. This matters as there is a strong body of research which suggests that, for example, teachers' self-reports of their behaviours and teaching styles are not particularly accurate and conflict with reports from external observers and from their students (Muijs, forthcoming). One reason for this is that it can be quite hard for people to reflect on and to know what they are actually doing. Many teachers have had little chance to compare their teaching to that of colleagues, which makes it hard for them to say whether or not they use a lot of group work in their teaching, for example. In some cases participants can be prone to give a *socially desirable response* in questionnaires. Imagine that you are evaluating a new government teaching strategy. The teacher would know that the 'right' answer to a question on her teaching would be the one that accords with the new teaching method, and might be tempted to answer this whether or not she actually used this method. Direct access to social situations is also often necessary when we are looking at children. Younger children may find it very difficult to answer questions on their interactions with peers, and even measuring their learning is often best done using observational methods, as using tests can be unreliable with young children.

■ Observational methods are varied and flexible. It is possible to observe a wide range of situations in a variety of ways. This means that, like survey research, we can look at quite a wide range of research questions using observational methods.

■ As we are observing in natural settings, we can more easily generalise our results to other real-life settings than when we use experimental methods.

However, observational research also has a number of important disadvantages.

■ The first is the high demands on time, effort and resources that this method makes. Observations are intense and time-consuming. The observation itself is time-consuming (e.g. a 50-minute lesson plus writing up), and in many cases we will want to observe the same pupils or teachers several times in order to ensure reliability. If we observe just the once, we wouldn't know whether the behaviour observed was typical or just a one-off. Observation also requires significant training for the observer, as it is important that the observer achieves reliability, i.e. if you observe the same situation twice, you would want to have the same results. This becomes even more important when we have more than one observer in a research project because we need to ensure that they use the same criteria when observing.

■ Observations are intrusive for those being observed who can often find the experience stressful and are therefore not necessarily keen to participate. This is certainly so in a situation where most observations are done by those in a position of power as a means of performance assessment or monitoring as is often the case in education. As a researcher you can help alleviate this by making sure that you explain that you are researching rather than monitoring and by smiling and appearing friendly when observing. As anyone who has been observed in any situation will know, however, it will not totally alleviate the problem.

■ The fact that observation is intrusive also means that the observer can easily influence the situation. If you were being observed you might be more nervous or try and behave in a more exemplary way than usual. Children can sometimes play up to outside observers, teachers can try and teach in the way they think observers want, prepare more for lessons that are to be observed and so on. There is not much one can realistically do about this as an observer other than to increase the number of observations so the observed become used to your presence. You will need to take into account that bias is being introduced by your presence as an observer. A second form of bias that may occur is observer bias, i.e. the fact that you as an observer may interpret things in a particular way. If more than one observer is taking part in the study, this problem is multiplied. This can only be overcome through training, practice and clear guidelines and criteria for the observation.

■ Finally, as observation, like survey research, is non-experimental, the same problems apply when trying to make causal inferences.

▪▪▪ Example 3.2

The relationship between teacher behaviours and pupil outcomes

This large-scale study into the effects of teacher behaviours on achievement in mathematics was carried out in primary schools in England (Muijs and Reynolds, 2002). As part of this study, over 100 teachers were observed each year, and their pupils given a standardised mathematics test at the start and the end of the year.

The observation schedules used contained a number of sections: observers gave a descriptive account of the lesson, noting the content and the main events throughout. They also noted whether the activity could be described as group work, individual work, whole-class lecture-style teaching or whole-class interactive teaching (transitions between parts of the lesson and admin were also noted). They scanned the classroom every five minutes, and counted the number of pupils on and off task. Following the lesson, observers completed a rating scale noting the occurrence of over 50 distinct teacher behaviours.

It was found that a large range of teacher behaviours were positively related to achievement in mathematics. These behaviours were also related to one another, forming an 'effective teaching' construct. Being taught by the most as opposed to the least effective teacher could make up to 20 per cent difference in test scores at the end of the year, taking into account scores at the start of the year and pupil background. It was also found that in classrooms where more whole-class interactive teaching was used teachers engaged in higher levels of effective behaviours than in classrooms where more individual work was used. Group work was seldom used in the classrooms observed, notwithstanding its positive effects where it was observed.

Designing observational studies

In essence, an observational study is structured in the same way as a survey study. The elements of designing research objectives, defining populations and sampling are similar. One difference is that in observational studies we are not just sampling respondents or settings, but slices of time (or occasions) as well. What do we mean by this? Basically, when doing an observation of a lesson, for example, what we often want to do is generalise our findings to all that teacher's lessons, or when we are observing children playing, we want to generalise the play behaviours we have observed to those children's general play. Therefore every observation is a sample from the population of possible lessons or playtimes. We are sampling twice: respondents from the population of respondents, and observations from the total of possible observations of those respondents. When taking a random sample, we will then effectively be taking two random samples from two populations, one of respondents and one of observations nested within the respondents.

Designing instruments is a crucial step in observation-based research, and there are a number of different ways in which we can design observation instruments. The main instrument in any observational research is of course the observation schedule, which can take on a number of different forms.

The easiest form to construct, but in many ways the most difficult to use and analyse, is the *descriptive observation record*. On a descriptive observation form, the observer is asked to write down everything relevant that is happening during the observed session, focusing obviously on those things germane to the research question, for example interactions between pupils in small groups. The open-ended and essentially qualitative nature of this format has the advantage that it allows observers to pick up factors that they haven't thought of beforehand (in contrast to scales), and that it can provide very detailed and rich information. Disadvantages are that this information is difficult and time-consuming to code, requires very high levels of alertness and concentration from observers, and can be difficult to compare across observations, especially where more than one observer is involved in the project. An example of a descriptive form is given in appendix 3.1 to this chapter, where the observer is asked to write down the main elements of an observed lesson and give the timing for each change that occurs. Subjectivity and bias can be a problem both in writing down observations and in coding them.

A more common method is to use a *rating scale* on which the observer can rate the occurrence or quality of observed factors. For example, one can rate the quality of interactions between teachers and pupils (see appendix 3.2 to this chapter). This type of rating scale is called a *high inference* observation instrument because it requires the observer to make a judgement on what is observed. This is contrasted with *low inference* instruments, where observers are just asked to count behaviours (for example, number of questions asked to boys and girls). Low inference measures obviously involve far less decision-making on the part of the observer, and are therefore more objective and unbiased as observer subjectivity is left out of the equation. On the other hand, this clearly limits what can be researched. It is easy to count the number of interactions with students that a teacher has during a particular session, but you can't count the quality of these interactions. Therefore, for many research questions, it will be necessary to use higher inference measures. As with rating scales in questionnaires, good observation rating scales are clear, unambiguous and do not contain too many scale points.

Time sampling entails taking a snapshot of an event at a given time interval (e.g. every five minutes). This is used, for example, when researchers want to measure time on task of pupils in a classroom. Every five or ten minutes, the researcher scans the room and counts who is visibly on or off task. A percentage on task for the lesson can then be calculated. When doing this you need to remember that you are sampling time points, and that a sufficiently large sample is necessary to ensure that you aren't just picking an untypical moment when pupils are being particularly well or badly behaved!

These different types of rating scales can be combined into one instrument to look at various factors, such as time on task and teacher behaviours, simultaneously. This can be done by using both a rating scale and a time on task count, although this obviously puts additional demands on the observer.

Collecting the data is done by observing a situation, setting or interaction using the constructed instrument. Observation is one of the most complex and exhausting forms of data collection, requiring a great deal of concentration and attentiveness. When observing you always have to remain focused on the elements you want to observe without getting distracted. When counting you may have to use time sampling if the behaviours you are counting occur frequently. When using a rating scale, it is often best to take descriptive notes and complete the ratings following the observation; otherwise you may have to change ratings as the observed session goes on (for example, the teacher may not ask a lot of open questions at the start of the lesson, but this may increase towards the end).

One question you may be confronted with during observations is whether or not to become involved in the session. In quantitative (as opposed to qualitative ethnographic) research we usually want to influence the setting we are observing as little as possible to avoid bias, and therefore it is recommended not to become involved. However, this is often easier said than done. In situations where you as an adult are observing young children they will often turn to you with questions and/or requests for help. While strictly scientifically one should not intervene, ethically I find it hard to turn away a child. This therefore is something of a judgement call. In any case, you should not get in the way of the teacher, or do anything the teacher doesn't want you to.

■ ■ ■ Analysing existing datasets

Instead of collecting our own data, we can often use existing datasets to look at particular educational questions. For example, we might want to look at which schools have improved most in terms of achievement over the past five years. In such an instance, we can use publicly available data, like state-mandated or national test results to see which schools have most increased their scores. There are also a number of datasets available which researchers can purchase for their own use. The National Education Longitudinal Studies (NELS) programme of the National Center for Education Statistics (NCES) provides interesting longitudinal data on the educational, vocational and personal development of young people in the US, beginning with their elementary or high school years and following them over time. The same organisation has also started a longitudinal study on early childhood. Datasets can be purchased from http://nces.ed.gov. Non-quantitative existing data can be coded for use in quantitative studies, for example data from inspection reports, in England freely available from Ofsted (the Office for Standards in Education), the official inspection body (www.ofsted.gov.uk). Data on school background (e.g. percentage of pupils with special needs) and size are contained in the documents, as are quantifiable judgements on the quality of various aspects of schooling.

When using official data, it is important to remember that the purposes for which they have been collected are often very different than those for which you might want to use them. Inspection data, for example, is not collected for research purposes and therefore may not be suitable for all studies. The reliability of the data is often unknown. Even with state-mandated tests psychometric properties aren't always published. Conditions of testing and data collection are not always clear to external researchers. These problems are far less acute with datasets collected for research purposes, such as the NCES studies, but even there you need to take into account that the way scales have been constructed and concepts defined may be different from how you as a researcher would want to define them. Also, most official data is, for obvious confidentiality reasons, published at the school level only (and not at the pupil level). This can lead to problems in interpretation and analysis, as aggregated figures may hide variance within the school. There are also statistical problems with such data which we will discuss in Chapter 11.

Nevertheless, existing datasets form an invaluable resource for educational researchers and can often be a cheap and efficient way of answering certain research questions.

While we have discussed these different methods separately, it can be a good idea to combine different types of research in one study. For example, when we want to look at what school and classroom factors influence achievement, we can combine existing student test data (for example, scores on state-mandated tests), results from a survey of head teachers on their management and leadership practices, and observation of teachers to look at teacher behaviours. Combining quantitative and qualitative data collection methods can often enrich our research. For example, if we want to know what factors distinguish particularly effective schools, we may wish to collect quantitative state-mandated test and pupil background data to identify highly effective schools, but then use qualitative interviews of staff members to look in depth at what these schools are doing to achieve these results.

The best advice I can give on choosing a research method for your study is to go for 'fitness for purpose', choosing the method best suited to answering your research question. The advantages and disadvantages of the various methods summarised above should help you do this.

■ ■ ■ Common misconceptions

1. *I want to study whether watching too much television causes low achievement in primary school pupils. I've collected test data and data from a questionnaire on children's TV viewing, and I've found a relationship between the two. That means that I can support my hypothesis and say that watching TV causes low achievement, right?* No. It is very hard to make firm conclusions on causation using survey research, and the fact that we have found a relationship doesn't prove anything in that respect. The relationship may be caused by a third, confounding variable (e.g. kids from lower socio-economic status backgrounds watch more TV and get lower grades at school), or causality may be in the other direction (kids who do badly at school experience lowered self-esteem from which they try to escape by watching more TV). One needs at least to do longitudinal research and collect a lot of data on possible confounding variables to be more sure, but at the end of the day experimental methods are better suited to determining causality.

2. *Survey research is the easiest kind of research to do.* Survey research may be the most efficient way of collecting large quantities of data, but designing a good survey study is by no means easy. Careful thought must be put into designing and testing the instruments, taking the sample and minimising non-response. Hastily and flippantly executed survey research is common and usually produces unreliable or trivial studies.

3. *Observational research is less biased than survey research because it allows us to see the world as it is.* That is only partly the case. While observational research does not rely on the perceptions of the respondent like survey research, it does rely on the perceptions of the observer, who may be biased in some way. Also, the mere presence of an external observer will change the way the people being observed behave. Therefore an observation is never a 'pure' picture of the world as it is.

■ ■ ■ Summary

Survey research is one of the most common research methods in social science and education. This is largely because it is an efficient way of collecting large amounts of data and is flexible in the sense that a large number of topics can be studied. However, the perception that doing survey research is easy is wrong. What the population is and how to sample from it need to be carefully considered as only probability samples are unbiased. Non-response is common and can also lead to bias in survey research, as can badly designed questionnaires. Avoiding double negatives, ambiguous or unclear questions, and double questions, keeping questionnaires brief and being culturally sensitive can help minimise bias.

Observational research can give direct access to social situations, which means we don't have to rely on respondent self-reporting; this is particularly important when researching areas in which there may be some socially desirable response bias. Observations are highly time-consuming, require a lot of training of observers and can be biased because the observer will inevitably influence the behaviour of those observed. Systematic observation entails developing observation instruments that can have a variety of forms. Descriptions of the observation give detailed information but are hard to code. Counts of particular behaviours are highly reliable but limit us in what we can observe. Rating scales solve that problem, but can be unreliable because they require more inference from the observer.

Finally, we can often use existing datasets such as state-mandated test data, inspection reports or publicly available educational datasets. While this is probably the most economical way of collecting data, we must remember that these datasets have been collected for different purposes than our research, and possibly with different definitions of key concepts. Reliability may also be unknown.

Combining several types of data can often help illuminate more complex research questions.

■ ■ ■ Exercises

1. What are the main differences between experimental and non-experimental studies?

2. 'Observational studies give us a true picture of reality, while surveys only give us perceptions.' Do you agree or disagree with this statement? Why?

3. If surveys are the most flexible and efficient way of doing research, why would we want to do any other kind of research?

4. I want to know whether teachers' classroom practice influences pupils' self-concept. Can you design a study that looks at this?

5. I want to know what both teachers and pupils in my school think of the new mentoring system I have introduced. Can you design a study that looks at this?

6. I want to know whether self-concept influences pupil achievement, or whether it is higher pupil performance that leads to a more positive self-concept. Is it possible to determine this using non-experimental research? If yes, how would you do that?

Appendix 3.1 Example of descriptive form

Time	Descriptive notes

Activity key: 1 = Whole class interactive   a = Calculators

2 = Whole class lecture   b = Collaborative

3 = Individual/group work

4 = Classroom management

Appendix 3.2 Rating the quality of interactions between teachers and pupils

1 = behaviour rarely observed

2 = behaviour occasionally observed

3 = behaviour often observed

4 = behaviour frequently observed

5 = behaviour consistently observed

na = not applicable

Provides students with review and practice

1. The teacher clearly explains tasks   1   2   3   4   5   na

2. The teacher offers effective assistance to   1   2   3   4   5   na
   individuals/groups

3. The teacher checks for understanding   1   2   3   4   5   na

4. The teacher or students summarise   1   2   3   4   5   na
   the lesson

5. The teacher re-teaches if error rate is high   1   2   3   4   5   na

6. The teacher is approachable for students   1   2   3   4   5   na
   with problems

■ ■ ■ Chapter 4

Validity, reliability and generalisability

Three key concepts in quantitative methods are validity, reliability and generalisability. All three have got to do with *measurement*. Whenever we are doing quantitative research, we are trying to measure something. We might, for example, want to look at students' achievement in history. Achievement is a concept that we will have to try to measure, using a test, essay or portfolio. We might want to measure teachers' self-esteem. We would use a self-esteem instrument to do this. Measurement supplies the numbers we use in quantitative analyses. The question that follows from this is how well are we measuring what we want to measure. If you were wanting to measure your weight, you'd want to be sure that:

1. you weren't measuring something else (such as height) instead; and that

2. whatever scale you were using wasn't completely erratic (e.g. gave you a different value every time you used it).

The same goes when we are trying to measure things in educational research. That is where *validity* (1) and *reliability* (2) come in to play.

We saw in the previous chapter that we will usually take a sample rather than study the whole population. When we do this, what we really want to be able to do is to say something about characteristics of the population rather than just our sample. This is called *generalising* from the sample to the population, and is another concept we will discuss in this chapter.

■ ■ ■ Validity

What is validity?

Validity asks the question: are we measuring what we want to measure? This may sound obvious but is often not that simple in educational research. Most of the concepts we want to measure, self-concept or attitudes for example, can't be measured directly. Self-esteem is an abstract concept which, in some ways, is brought into existence by being measured. We cannot plug directly into people's heads and know what they are thinking, feeling or experiencing. It is in that sense a *latent variable* – a variable that can't be directly measured. Therefore we need to develop instruments that measure these concepts indirectly, by using a questionnaire for example. Every question then becomes a *manifest variable* (a variable we actually measure) designed to tease out an underlying latent concept. Creating the right measurement instrument with the right manifest measures of the latent concept is clearly of crucial importance and not necessarily easy to achieve. The same is the case for concepts that may at first sight seem more straightforward. One of the mainstays of quantitative educational research is of course the achievement test. This is often used in an unproblematic way as an outcome measure in educational studies (e.g. what school characteristics affect achievement?). The question, though, is what do we want to measure? Often we want to make some broader comment about pupils' ability or achievement in a subject or, even more broadly, about their learning. After all, the actual goal of educational endeavour is learning, not scores on a particular achievement test. Learning, like self-esteem, cannot be measured directly. Again, to be able to do that we would need to plug directly into people's brains and see what has actually happened there. Tests, essays and whatever other measure we use are always indirect measures of learning. Whether they are good measures is hotly disputed. Are the tests too narrow? Are they measuring higher-order skills, or only basic skills? All these questions relate directly to the validity of the test.

This means that validity is probably the single most important aspect of the design of any measurement instrument in educational research. However good our research design or sophisticated our statistical analyses, the results will be meaningless if we aren't actually measuring what we are purporting to measure.

Types of validity

Validity has three distinct aspects, all of which are important. They are: *content validity*, *criterion validity* and *construct validity*.

Content validity

Content validity refers to whether or not the content of the manifest variables (e.g. items of a test or questions of a questionnaire) is right to measure the latent concept (self-esteem, achievement, attitudes,...) that we are trying to measure. For example, if we were trying to measure pupils' attitudes to school, we couldn't ask 'how do you get on with your parents?' More difficult to determine would be an item like: 'My teachers always try to help me'. Would this be a valid measure of attitudes to school, or are attitudes to teachers something different?

Clearly there is an important role for theory in determining content validity. The better we know our subject and how the concepts we are using are theoretically defined, the better we will be able to design an instrument that is content-valid. The main judgement of whether an instrument is content valid is therefore its accordance to a theory of how the concept works and what it is.

An extensive search of the literature on the concept you are wanting to measure is going to help you to achieve content validity. Asking respondents whether the instrument or test looks valid to them is also important. This is called establishing *face validity*, because respondents are judging whether the instrument looks OK to them. Setting up a panel of users and getting them to comment on your instrument while you are developing it is a good way of doing this. One problem with face validity is that lay users may not be fully cognisant of the theoretical background or subtlety of the concept, especially where you are using a psychological measure, for example. In that case it can be useful to have a panel of experts in the field judge your instrument as well. Using a panel of experts does not mean you shouldn't also look at face validity. After all, what the people who are actually going to complete your instrument think about it is going to affect how they respond to the questions.

Criterion validity

Like content validity, criterion validity is closely related to theory. When you are developing a measure, you usually expect it – in theory at least – to be related to other measures or to predict certain outcomes. For example, if we develop a new mathematics test, we would expect the scores pupils achieve on that test not to be totally unrelated to those they get on a state-mandated mathematics test.

There are two main types of criterion validity: *predictive validity* and *concurrent validity*.

Predictive validity refers to whether or not the instrument you are using predicts the outcomes you would theoretically expect it too. For example, when we select students to study on our university courses, we will use their scores on specific tests (e.g. SAT) to determine whether or not they are likely to successfully complete the course and are therefore suitable candidates. Any test we use for this purpose should therefore predict academic success. Likewise, whenever we develop a screening test for selection of employees, we expect this test to predict how well the prospective employee will do the job. Establishing whether or not this is the case will determine whether or not out measure has predictive validity.

Concurrent validity makes a less stringent assumption. The question here is whether scores on your instrument agree with scores on other factors you would expect to be related to it. For example, if you were to measure attitudes to school, you would, from theory, expect some relationship with school achievement. Likewise, when designing a measure of pupil learning in geography, you would expect there to be a relationship with scores on previously existing measures of learning in that subject.

What is needed to establish criterion validity are two things: a good knowledge of theory relating to the concept so that we can decide what variables we can expect to be predicted by and related to it, and a measure of the relationship between our measure and those factors. To do the latter we need first of all to collect data on those factors from the same respondents we are measuring with our new instrument, and secondly to statistically measure whether there is a relationship using techniques such as the correlation coefficient (see Chapter 8).

Construct validity

Construct validity is a slightly more complex issue relating to the internal structure of an instrument and the concept it is measuring. Once again, this is related to our theoretical knowledge of the concept we are wanting to measure. We might hypothesise that our concept or achievement measure has a number of different dimensions. For example, a test of mathematics ability might include items relating to number, shape and space, etc. We would then want to know whether all the items relate to the right dimension (e.g. an item that we have designed to measure number should measure number and not shape and space, or a combination of the two).

An example might help to clarify this. We might want to look at a measure of pupil self-concept. Desk research (looking at the literature on self-concept) suggests that this is a multidimensional construct. We can have different self-concepts in different areas. For example, I might have a positive self-concept of myself as a quantitative researcher but a far more negative one of myself as a cook. The same goes for primary school age children. Shavelson (1976) hypothesised that among children and adolescents seven dimensions were the most important: self-concept of school subjects, self-concept of English, self-concept of mathematics, self-concept of relations with peers (other children), self-concept of relations with parents, self-concept of appearance and self-concept of athletic ability. These factors are arranged in the mind in a hierarchical manner, meaning that the three school-related factors go together to form an *academic self-concept* (e.g. I'm generally a good student) while the other four factors go together to form a *non-academic self-concept*. These then form the overall or global self-concept, as depicted in Figure 4.1.

If we want to measure self-concept according to this model, we will want to develop a measure that includes questions on all seven subscales. We would then want to be sure that items that were supposed to measure peer relations self-concept measured that subscale and not body image self-concept. To do this we can use a statistical method called confirmatory factor analysis (part of structural equation modelling) which we will look at in Chapter 11. This will tell us whether each item measures the subscale it is supposed to measure and not any other.

Obviously, in some cases we might not hypothesise that our construct had multiple subscales. It could be that we only wanted to measure one very specific aspect. In that case all items would have to measure that

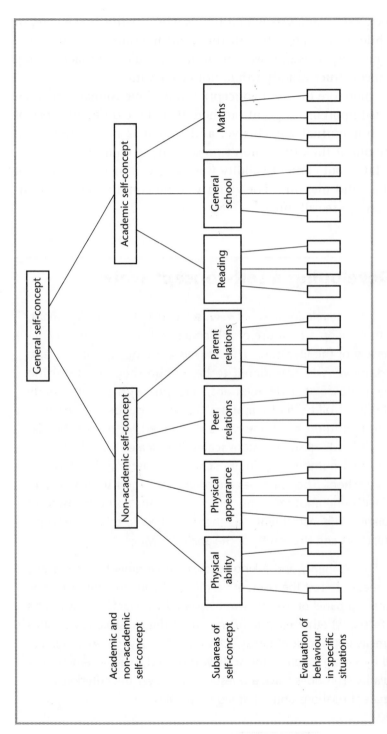

■ **Figure 4.1**
Shavelson's multifaceted, hierarchical self-concept model.

Source: H. W. Marsh and R. J. Shavelson (2985) 'Self-concept: its multifaceted heirarchical structure', *Educational Psychologist*, 20, 114. Copyright © 1985 Lawrence Erlbaum Associates.

one construct. Factor analysis would tell us whether this is the case, or whether, while we thought that all the items measure one construct, they in fact measure several. If we were to measure a certain factor using just one item construct validity would not be relevant.

Validity is therefore (like self-concept) a multidimensional construct. However, it is important to point out here that these different types of validity are not mutually exclusive, and that it is not sufficient to demonstrate one if the others aren't present. If we could demonstrate construct validity but content validity was not clear, then we could not say we had a valid measure. For validity to be convincingly demonstrated, we have to see all three.

■ ■ ■ Developing a self-concept scale

For a study into the relationship between self-concept and achievement, I decided to develop a measure of self-concept. I started with a wide-ranging review of the literature. The Shavelson model of self-concept, mentioned above, was considered to be a good theoretical starting point. Seven subscales: peer relations, relations with parents, body image, physical ability, mathematics, Dutch language and general school were hypothesised. Items were developed for each subscale, based on existing English-language scales. The scales thus developed were shown to a number of primary school teachers, and tested in a local primary school. The scale was factor analysed, and subscales were correlated with one another, achievement in maths and a measure of peer popularity. The instrument was then changed to reflect the comments of teachers and the results of the analyses (Muijs, 1997).

The grounding in theory and asking teachers to comment on the scale, were both meant to test the content validity of the instrument. An omission was that no panel of experts was convened. The factor analysis was designed to see whether each item measured the subscale it was supposed to measure to look at construct validity. Finally, criterion validity was tested by seeing whether the scale was related to achievement and peer popularity. This does leave a question mark over the criterion validity of the parent relations and self-image subscales.

■ ■ ■ Reliability

What is reliability?

A second element that determines the quality of our measurement instruments is *reliability*. We all know the meaning of the word reliability outside of quantitative research. Our car is reliable if it doesn't break down. Our boy/girlfriends are unreliable because they are always late when we are supposed to meet up. In measurement, reliability is a key concept. If you were on a diet and wanted to measure your weight to see whether the diet was having any effect, you'd want to be certain that the scales you were using were measuring your weight accurately and would not decide to add a few pounds on one day and take of a few the next day in a random way. The same is true if we are measuring concepts like academic achievement or teacher behaviours in educational research.

Reliability does have a specific meaning when we are talking about statistical measurement. Basically, whenever we are measuring something, there is some element of error called *measurement error*. Reliability then refers to the extent to which test scores are free of measurement error. Any score we get on a test or scale will have three main elements:

Score = True score + Systematic error + Random error

The true score is what we really want to measure, the score without any error. Systematic error is error that is the same from one measurement to the next. For example, if we are measuring weight using a weighing scale, it may be that we have calibrated our scale so that it starts at 2 rather than 0 kg. Every time you measured yourself, you would be two kilos too heavy. This would not be a problem if we knew what the fault was – we could simply subtract two from every measurement we got. If we don't know what the systematic error is, our measurement will become less valid. Reliability has to do with the second part of error, unsystematic or random error. This is error that will fluctuate from one measurement to the next and that is unpredictable. This type of error is usually quite limited in scientific measurement instruments but can be quite substantial in educational measurement. Think, for example, of a school achievement test. A whole lot of elements can cause our tests to be less reliable, resulting in random error. An item may be worded in a way that can lead to confusion, or it may be too difficult, leading to guessing. Even more random elements can intervene: the mood of the pupil when taking the test, the temperature in the room and so on. Obviously, while both can lead to unreliability, the first set is the one we can actually do something about when developing our instrument. The second set of factors we may be able to do something about when administering our instrument, but that is an element of research design rather than instrument design.

Unreliability is clearly a problem. If we measure something unreliably our results are untrustworthy and any conclusions tainted. Unreliable instruments will also lead to relationships with other variables being lower than if they were more reliable, thus harming our ability to come to clear research findings. Low reliability of our instruments is one of the reasons why many of the relationships we find in educational research are low.

Types of reliability

Reliability, as conceptualised in quantitative research, has two main forms: *repeated measurement* and *internal consistency*.

Repeated measurement has to do with our ability to measure the same thing at different times. As mentioned above, it would not do if our instrument randomly came up with different scores every time we used it. The same instrument should come up with the same answer when used with the same respondent. In order to see whether our measures are reliable in that respect, we can simply use them with the same respondents and see whether the answers they give haven't changed too much. This is called the *test-retest* method. One question that follows when using the test-retest method is how much time we need to let go by before retesting. This is difficult to answer. If we leave too little time, then respondents might remember how they answered last time and simply give the same answer because of this. This is called a *carryover* effect and can lead to us overestimating the reliability of the test. However, if we leave too long between test and retest, the respondents' attitudes or opinions might have genuinely changed, or where we are using an achievement test, the respondent may have (hopefully!) learned in the meantime. This can lead to us underestimating the reliability of our instrument. One to two weeks is often recommended as an optimal time, though the risk of some carryover effect remains.

When we have tested and retested we need to look at how strong the relationship is between the scores on the instrument at the two time points. To do this we can use a correlation coefficient (see Chapter 8). This needs to be as high as possible. Above 0.7 is usually considered to offer reasonable reliability for research purposes. When we want to make a high-stakes decision on the basis of the test (such as pass or fail on an exam), we would want to have a test-retest reliability of over 0.8.

A different form of repeated measurement is *inter-rater reliability*. This becomes important where we use more than one judge to look at a situation, such as where we have several classroom observers doing classroom observations. We would then want our observers to give the same rating to an event they had all observed. (For example, if we asked three observers to observe the same lesson and then to rate an item like 'the teacher asks open-ended questions' we wouldn't want three different ratings!) Whether this is the case can be tested simply by doing it in practice and then comparing the responses of all the raters.

The second form of reliability is *internal consistency reliability*. This form of reliability is only applicable to instruments that have more than one item as it refers to how homogeneous the items of a test are or how well they measure a single construct. When developing our self-concept scale, for example, we could first see whether the seven subscales we hypothesise exist and are measured by the variables we thought they would be (testing construct validity). Then for each subscale we can look at whether the items measure it in a reliable, internally homogeneous way.

There are two main ways of calculating internal consistency reliability: *split half reliability* and *coefficient alpha*. Split half reliability works as follows: say we have an attitude to teaching measure that consists of 10 items. First, we randomly split the test into two (for example, the even and uneven items). Then we calculate respondents' scores on each 'half test'. We can then see whether the two scores are related to one another. If they are both measuring the same thing, we would expect them to be strongly related, with a correlation coefficient of over 0.8. Coefficient alpha is another measure of internal consistency. We would expect this measure to be over 0.7 before we can say that our test is internally consistent.

When we measure internal consistency or test-retest reliability, we may find that our test is not in fact reliable enough. Then we need to see whether we can pinpoint any particular item as being 'at fault'. When looking at internal consistency, we can look at how strongly each individual item is correlated with the scale score. Any items that are weakly related to the test as a whole lower our reliability and should be removed from our instrument. When looking at test-retest reliability, we can identify items that respondents are scoring very differently on at our two test times. These are causing lower reliability.

What can we do to make our instruments more reliable? A lot of this has to do with simply ensuring that the quality of questions we ask is high and unambiguous (see the previous chapter). Unambiguous and clear questions are likely to be more reliable, and the same goes for items on a rating scale for observers.

Another way to make an instrument more reliable is by measuring it with more than one item. When we use more than one item, individual errors that respondents can make when answering a single item (misreading a question, for example) cancel each other out. That is why we construct scales. In general, more items means higher reliability. We don't necessarily want to take this to extremes, though. Respondents can get bored if you keep on asking them what seem like similar questions, and are then likely to start filling out questions without concentrating and in an increasingly haphazard way. This will increase the risk of measurement error rather than reducing it. Also, as we saw in the previous chapter, we want to keep survey instruments short, and if we use scales with a lot of items, we won't be able to ask about many different things. For most attitude type scales, somewhere between four and ten items will lead to sufficient reliability. For achievement tests you might want more items because of the high-stakes nature of these tests.

A final way of making instruments more reliable is to measure a construct that is very clearly and even narrowly defined. This may in some cases conflict with validity (are we measuring our concepts too narrowly?). Obviously we want to try and create measurements that are both reliable and valid. Remember, though, that there is not much point in creating an instrument that is reliably measuring something we don't really want to measure!

■ ■ ■ Generalisability

As we saw in Chapter 2, we often have to take a sample of our population rather than measure the population itself. We will then do the research with our sample. When we do this, the results we find strictly speaking relate only to that sample. Usually, we will want to generalise our findings to the population. When I am looking at the relationship between teacher behaviours and pupil achievement, I don't just want to be able to say something about what the 100 teachers in my sample do that affects their pupils. I would really like to say something about behaviours of teachers more generally – in other words, generalise to the population.

Probability and statistical significance

Generalising to the population is not something we can just automatically go out and do, however. We saw in Chapter 2 that samples are often not totally representative of the population. Results we find in our sample might be a coincidence of that sample rather than existing within the population. For example, we may find a relationship between the use of a reward system by teachers and pupil achievement. But if we have only observed ten teachers this may just be because one particularly effective teacher in our sample happens to use a reward system in her lessons.

Therefore, whenever we find a relationship in our sample, this relationship may or may not exist in our population. We would like to be able to say with a certain *probability* how likely it is that we have found a relationship in our sample if it didn't exist in the population.

If you remember in Chapter 2 we looked at the issue of hypotheses. We said that there were two possible hypotheses, the null hypothesis and the alternative hypothesis. In this case, where we have looked at the relationship between the use of a reward system in a class and the performance of pupils in that class, the hypotheses might be the following:

- The null hypothesis is: there <u>is no</u> relationship between use of a reward system and pupil performance in the population.
- The alternative hypothesis is: there <u>is</u> a relationship between use of a reward system and pupil performance in the population.

In our study, we have observed our sample of ten teachers and found a relationship between the two. If, on the basis of this finding, we accept that there is a relationship in the population as well as in our sample, two situations can occur:

1. There is a relationship in the population. In that case we have correctly rejected the null hypothesis.
2. There is not a relationship in the population. In that case we have wrongly rejected the null hypothesis. This is called a *type I error*.

If, on the basis of finding a relationship in the sample, we decide that there is *not* a relationship in the population (because our relationship is only weak, for example), again two situations may occur:

1. There is indeed no relationship in the population. We have correctly accepted the null hypothesis.
2. There is a relationship in the population. In that case we have incorrectly rejected the null hypothesis. This is called a *type II error*.

If we depict this graphically, this gives us the possibilities shown in Figure 4.2.

What we will try to do is minimise our chances of making a type I or type II error. One way to do that is by increasing our sample size. We saw that errors can occur in small samples due to the influence of a small number of extreme cases (called *outliers*). The larger our sample, the less influential these unusual cases will be. Therefore a larger sample will decrease our chances of making both type I and type II errors.

		The real situation (in the population)	
		H_0 is true	H_1 is true
Your decision (based on the sample)	H_0 is supported	No error	Type II error
	H_1 is supported	Type I error	No error

▓ **Figure 4.2**
Type I and type II errors.

Given equal sample size, however, our chance of making a type I or type II error is inversely related: the larger our probability of making a type I error, the smaller our probability of making a type II error. There is a trade-off between the two.

What then do we need to do? Which of the two error types is more important – which one do we most want to minimise? Imagine a situation where we have developed a new teaching method and want to test whether this is improving pupil outcomes. If we develop a quasi-experimental study in a random sample of schools to test this, our null hypothesis would be: the new teaching method does not improve achievement. The alternative hypothesis would be: the new teaching method does improve achievement. If, on the basis of our research, we reject the null hypothesis, two situations can occur:

1. The alternative hypothesis is true in the population. We have no error.
2. The null hypothesis is true in the population. We have a type I error.

If we decide on the basis of results from our sample to accept the null hypothesis the following two situations can occur:

1. The null hypothesis is true in the population. We have no error.
2. The alternative hypothesis is true in the population. We have a type II error.

What are the consequences of the two types of error? The consequence of a type II error in this case is that we would decide not to use a promising teaching strategy, depriving pupils of the chance to benefit from it. The consequence of making a type I error is that we would change our teaching methods, at great cost and effort for teachers and the education system, causing upheaval to pupils with no discernible benefit. The latter is generally considered the more serious, so what we want to do is minimise our type I error. Another reason for this is that the alternative hypothesis is usually the one we, the researchers, want to be true. This will make it tempting for us to conclude that there is a relationship. In order to stop this 'wishful thinking' from distorting the results of scientific studies, a conservative approach, whereby the onus is on disproving the null hypothesis (the one we don't want), is necessary. Obviously having as small a type II error as possible is also important and therefore having a large sample is always advisable.

This means that wherever possible we will try to minimise the chance that we are making a type I error. To do that, we need to be able to calculate how large that chance is. That chance is given by the *level of significance*, also known as coefficient *alpha* (the chance of making a type II error is known as beta) or the *p(robability)-value*.

Throughout the rest of this book we will constantly be calculating p-values (or alphas or significant levels) using *significance tests*. In all cases these denote the *chance of committing a type I error*, which we will want to keep as small as possible. This significance level can vary between 0 and 1. The <u>smaller</u> our significance level, the <u>smaller</u> our chance of making a type I error. There are a number of standard values that are commonly used as cut-off points for the significance level. The most common is the 0.05 level. When we say the significance level is <u>less than</u> 0.05, this means that the probability that we would find the value we have in our sample if there was no relationship in the population is <u>less than</u> 5 per cent. In that case we usually say that our findings are *significant*. The word significant therefore has a different meaning in statistics than in daily life. It does not mean important. In some cases, when we have a large sample, we will use the 0.01 or 0.001 cut-off points. In the former case, the probability of finding a relationship between two variables (for example using a reward system and achievement) in our sample if there was not also a relationship in our population is less than 1 per cent. In the latter it is less than 0.01 per cent. Obviously, these cut-off points are arbitrary, and in that sense we need to be careful not to reify them, even though that is often what happens in quantitative research.

There are two things that determine the size of our significance level:

■ the size of the relationship or difference we have found in our sample; and
■ the size of our sample.

The latter is important to remember, as it means that the significance level p only tells us the probability that the relationship in our sample would exist if there was no relationship in the population. It does <u>not</u> tell us how strong our relationship is. A smaller p-value does not mean we have a stronger relationship, as it may result purely from an increase in the sample size.

An alternative view: effect size indices

Recently, there has been increasing criticism of the use of significance tests in statistics. These focus on a number of problems with the practice of significance testing.

One of these involves the use of arbitrary cut-off points like < 0.05, and indeed it can be argued that in many cases the difference between a significance level of 0.051 (not significant) and 0.049 (significant) is literally a couple of respondents. This must lead us to be cautious about interpreting the result of such analyses.

A further criticism is the fact that the null hypothesis, as above, is almost always interpreted to literally mean a difference of zero or no relationship in the population. There are two problems with this. One is that very few relationships are <u>exactly</u> 0. There is usually some element of relationship or difference present (this is known as the 'universal crud factor'). Therefore, given a sufficiently large sample, most relationships or differences between variables that we study will be statistically significant. They might, however, be so small as to be to all intents and purposes entirely trivial. If, for example, we had developed a new teaching method and it improved pupils' test scores by 0.01 per cent, we might well wonder whether it was worth pursuing. However, if we took a large enough sample (100,000 pupils, say) we might find it to be statistically significant, and some researchers might conclude that it is therefore important and worth pursuing. The second problem is that while we almost always test a hypothesis of no (zero) difference, in many cases this might be an absurd hypothesis. We might, for example, want to study the performance of students with special needs on a reading measure compared to that of students without special needs. All previous research tells us that they will perform less well than students with special needs. Therefore why test this yet again? We are much more likely to want to know whether the difference is larger than a certain amount. This is not a problem with hypotheses as such, because we have seen in

Chapter 2 that we can develop hypotheses that revolve around particular values rather than just no relationship versus a relationship. However, most statistical tests that are readily available in statistical packages (such as SPSS) only test the zero difference null hypothesis.

A number of remedies have been proposed for these problems. Some authors advocate not using any significance tests at all. They claim that the use of significance tests is holding back the development of social science, and they should be replaced by confidence intervals and effect sizes. The total abolition of significance testing remains a minority view, though, and most researchers still use significance testing. The counter argument to the abolitionist view remains that we must somehow decide whether our sample parameters, which will contain measurement error, are unusual enough for us to say that they are likely to result from actual population differences. Most researchers now do admit that the significance test has significant problems associated with it and should not be the sole measure we use.

Two main additional measures are proposed: one is the replacement of significance tests by confidence intervals. Confidence intervals give us a higher and lower bound between which our value (relationship, difference, mean,...) can fluctuate, given that we can never be certain what the exact value in the population is. We can say with a predetermined level of probability (e.g. 95 per cent) that given the value we have found, the value in the population is likely to vary between a minimum and a maximum value. For example, we could have found a mean of 76, and a 95 per cent confidence interval of between 72.5 and 80.5. This would mean that while in our sample the mean is 76, in the population it could be anywhere between 72.5 and 80.5 with a probability of 95 per cent. If we had a stricter probability level (e.g. 99 per cent), our estimate might vary between 65 and 86. Also, if we had a larger sample, our confidence interval would be narrower. The confidence interval therefore gives an indication of how much uncertainty there is in our estimate of the true value. The narrower the interval, the more precise is our estimate. At present confidence intervals are not as a rule produced in the output of most procedures in statistical software packages and are for that reason not used that often.

Another measure that is being increasingly used is the effect size. I mentioned above that the significance level does not tell us how strong our relationship, effect or difference is because this is to a large extent determined by the sample size. Effect size indices solve this problem by giving us a measure of the strength of our difference or relationship that we can then compare with results from other studies. This would allow us, for example, to say whether or not our new teaching strategy was having more effect on pupil outcomes than a rival method. It is clear that the use of effect sizes provides us with very important information when doing statistical analysis, and it is not surprising that more and more journals are requesting these measures from authors.

Obviously one important approach is simply to treat measures of significance with the necessary caution and look at them in conjunction with sample size and other measures rather than objectify and deify cut-off points. In this book I will present both measures of significance and measures of effect size whenever we are doing any kind of test. This is partly because I believe both measures give us useful information, and partly because, pragmatically, these are the measures you are likely to be asked to provide when you do statistical analyses.

■ ■ ■ Common misconceptions

1. *If we have a very low significance level, that means our result is important, doesn't it?* No. The significance level is determined both by the size of the relationship or difference and by the sample size. A very significant result may just mean that you have a large sample.

2. *But if I have a large effect size, then I can say that my findings are important, can't I?* No. Neither significance levels or effect sizes tell us whether our findings are important. This will be determined by their practical value or value to research and theory development. The effect size will be able to tell us whether the difference or relationship we have found is strong or weak.

3. *Aren't internal consistency reliability and construct validity the same thing?* No, not entirely, although they are related. Construct validity refers to cases where we have several subscales in our study and allows us to see whether our hypothesised structure works. Internal consistency reliability looks at every subscale or scale separately, and determines whether or not the items that make up that subscale are measuring the same thing.

▶

4. *If our results are significant, this means that they exist in the population, doesn't it?* This is not necessarily true. What the significance level is saying is that a result (relationship or difference) of the size we have found in the sample has a low probability of having occurred if there is no relationship in the population. However, there is still a probability (of 5 per cent, if we are using a significance level of 0.05, for example), that our findings are a coincidence of the sample. This probability level only holds if we have sampled randomly.

▪ ▪ ▪ Summary

In this chapter we have looked at a number of key concepts in quantitative methods: validity, reliability and generalisability. Validity basically concerns whether we are measuring what we want to measure and is probably the single most important aspect of measurement. There are three main types of validity: content validity, criterion validity and construct validity. Content validity refers to whether or not the content of the manifest variables (e.g. items of a test or questions of a questionnaire) is right to measure the latent concept (self-esteem, achievement, attitudes, ...) that you are trying to measure. Content validity is obviously related to your (theoretical) knowledge of the area, but can be improved by asking experts and respondents about their views on the content of the instrument. Your instrument can also theoretically be expected to predict or be related to other measures. If you collect information on these other measures you can determine this. This is criterion validity. Finally, you can design your instrument so that it contains several factors, rather than just one. The extent to which the data fit that theory is called construct validity.

Reliability refers to the extent to which test scores are free of measurement error. There are two types of reliability: repeated measures or test-retest reliability is about whether or not the instrument we use can be relied upon to give us similar results if used with the same respondents after a short period of time. Internal consistency refers to whether all the items are measuring the same construct.

In quantitative research we often want to generalise from our sample to the population. When we find a certain relationship or difference in our sample, we want to know whether this is because there is a difference in the population, or whether this is a coincidence or idiosyncrasy of our sample. We can never be 100 per cent sure of this, but we can calculate the probability that our relationship would occur if there was no difference in the population. When this probability is less than 0.05 (5 per cent), we say that the finding is statistically significant. The concept of significance testing has come under increasing criticism recently The cut-off points are seen as arbitrary, the reliance on a hypothesis of no difference in the population as unrealistic and the lack of information on the strength of the effect as unhelpful. For these reasons, many researchers have suggested replacing or supplementing significance level estimates with confidence intervals and effect size measures.

■ ■ ■ Exercises

1. What can you do to make your instrument more valid?
2. What do you think about the effect size vs. significance test debate: should we stick with significance levels, or replace them by effect size indices and confidence intervals?
3. How would you calculate whether or not your test was reliable?
4. Do you think a more reliable test is automatically more valid?
5. What types of error can you make when accepting the alternative hypothesis?
6. How can you make your instruments more reliable?

■ ■ ■ Further reading

Pedhazur, E. J. and Pedhazur Schmelkin, L. (1991) *Measurement, Design and Analysis* (Hillsdale, NJ: Lawrence Erlbaum) gives a comprehensive overview of issues of reliability and validity, as well as other elements of quantitative analysis.

A good practical guide to reliability and validity in survey research in particular is provided in Litwin, M. S. (1995) *How to Measure Survey Reliability and Validity* (Sage Publications).

Chapter 1 in Wonnacott, T. H. and Wonnacott, R. J. (1990) *Introductory Statistics* (New York: John Wiley) provides an overview of probability and significance testing.

The arguments on significance testing rehearsed by authors supporting each side of the debate are explored in Harlow, L. L., Mulaik, S. A. and Steiger, J. (1997. *What If There Were No Significance Tests?* (Mahwah, NJ: Lawrence Erlbaum). This is an excellent book but quite a technical read.

■ ■ ■ Chapter 5

Introduction to SPSS and the dataset

I mentioned in Chapter 1 that nowadays, rather than having to calculate the mathematical equations for our data analysis ourselves, we will usually get software packages to do this. There is a variety of packages out there that do quantitative data analysis.

SAS, BMDP, Stata, Splus and GBStat are all general purpose statistical analysis software packages. Excel and other spreadsheet software allow quantitative data analysis (Excel has an 'analysis tool-pak' add-on module), although these are more limited in scope and often less user-friendly than the specialised packages. In this book we are going to use SPSS. This because SPSS is probably the most common statistical data analysis software package used in educational research and is available at most institutions of higher education. It is also quite user-friendly and does everything we need it to do. This does not mean that it is necessarily 'better' than any of the other packages. Other packages may be better in some areas, but SPSS is by far the most commonly used statistical data analysis software. SPSS is a Windows-based program, and shares many features with other Windows-based software. A Mac version is also available.

■ ■ ■ Introduction to SPSS

Let's have a look what SPSS is like. When we open SPSS, we get the screen shown in Figure 5.1. We can see that the screen is dominated by a grid. This is where (once we have opened a file) we will find the variables and the units. Our units are the rows, numbered from 1 to however many people we have in our study. The variables are the columns. The names appear at the top of the grid (where it now says 'var').

The top row has a number of names, like 'file', 'edit', 'view' and so on. Many of these will be familiar to users of other Windows-based software like Word, and they fulfil the same functions in SPSS. Others ('Data', 'Transform', 'Analyze', etc.) are different. This is where we will find our data analysis tools which we will be discussing in the next chapters.

Below that is another row of symbols. Again some of these will be familiar to you from other Windows-based programs. Others launch SPSS-specific methods.

Opening a datafile is pretty much the same as in a program like Word or Excel. We simply need to go into the Open folder icon, and select our file, called 'quants file'. (Remember, you can download that file from the website as instructed in the preface.)

Now we can see that the values for all variables for every unit have appeared in the grid (see Figure 5.2). The value of the variable 'age' for respondent (unit) 1 is 123, for example (age is calculated in months here).

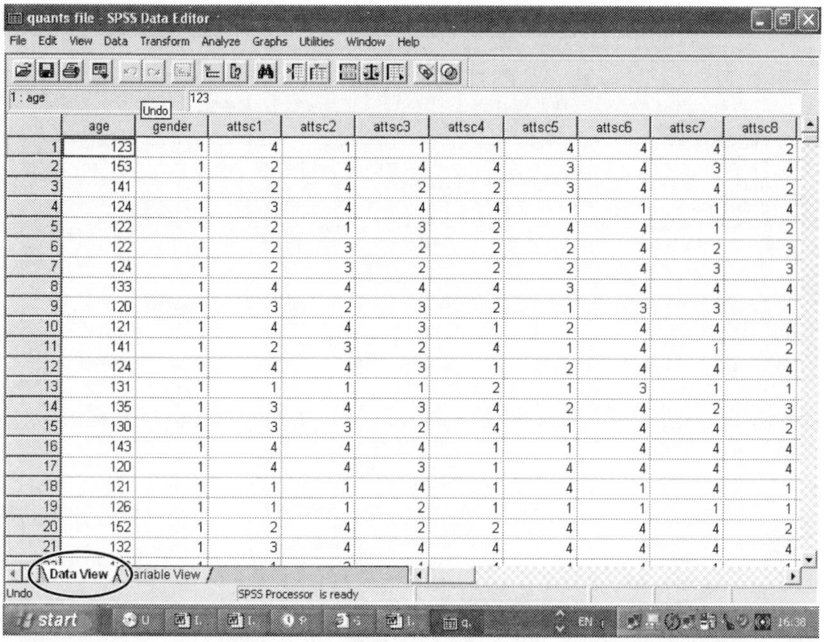

■ **Figure 5.2**
The 'Data View' screen with our file opened.

While we can see the names of all the variables along the top of the grid, these are not necessarily very clear. What does 'attsc 1' mean? Couldn't we have given longer, more explanatory names? Well, one problem with SPSS is that the length of a variable name can only be eight characters, which doesn't give us that much scope for clarity. Luckily, we can add some explanation, and I have done that for the variables in this sample. To see the explanation, we need to go into a different screen, however.

How do we do that? Well, at the bottom of the screen you will see two tabs, one called 'Data View' the other 'Variable View'. What we need to do is go into 'Variable View' by clicking on that tab.

Once we have done this, we can see a new screen (see Figure 5.3). which lists, in the first column, the names of all the variables in our file. The next columns list other variable characteristics, like type (numeric (numbers), string (letters) and so on), width of the variable and number of decimal points. The next column gives us the labels. This is where we can find out what the variable actually means. So, for example, our variable 'attsc 1' is

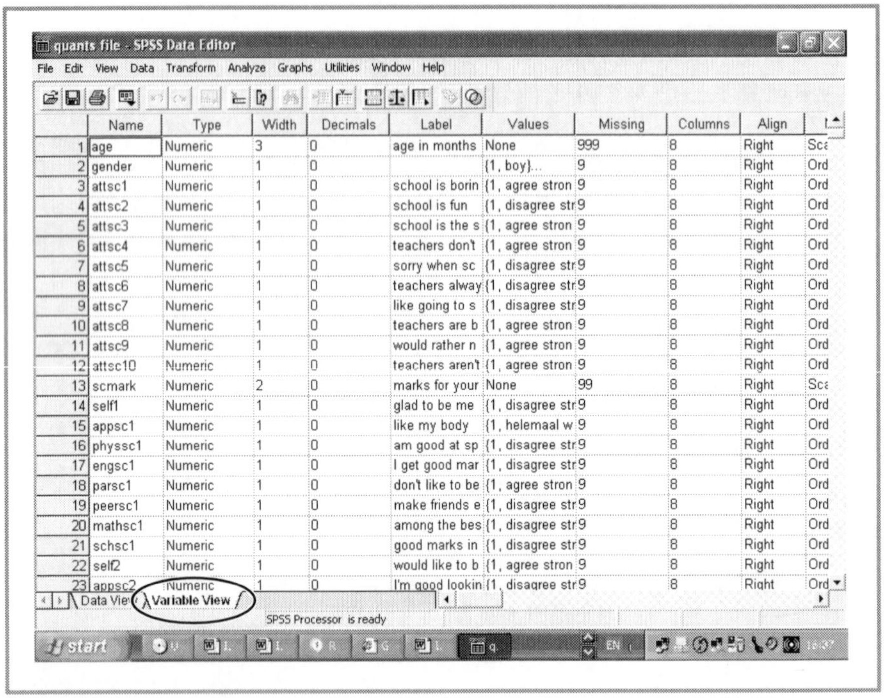

	Name	Type	Width	Decimals	Label	Values	Missing	Columns	Align	M
1	age	Numeric	3	0	age in months	None	999	8	Right	Sca
2	gender	Numeric	1	0		{1, boy}...	9	8	Right	Ord
3	attsc1	Numeric	1	0	school is borin	{1, agree stron	9	8	Right	Ord
4	attsc2	Numeric	1	0	school is fun	{1, disagree str	9	8	Right	Ord
5	attsc3	Numeric	1	0	school is the s	{1, agree stron	9	8	Right	Ord
6	attsc4	Numeric	1	0	teachers don't	{1, agree stron	9	8	Right	Ord
7	attsc5	Numeric	1	0	sorry when sc	{1, disagree str	9	8	Right	Ord
8	attsc6	Numeric	1	0	teachers alway	{1, disagree str	9	8	Right	Ord
9	attsc7	Numeric	1	0	like going to s	{1, disagree str	9	8	Right	Ord
10	attsc8	Numeric	1	0	teachers are b	{1, agree stron	9	8	Right	Ord
11	attsc9	Numeric	1	0	would rather n	{1, agree stron	9	8	Right	Ord
12	attsc10	Numeric	1	0	teachers aren't	{1, agree stron	9	8	Right	Ord
13	scmark	Numeric	2	0	marks for your	None	99	8	Right	Sca
14	self1	Numeric	1	0	glad to be me	{1, disagree str	9	8	Right	Ord
15	appsc1	Numeric	1	0	like my body	{1, helemaal w	9	8	Right	Ord
16	physsc1	Numeric	1	0	am good at sp	{1, disagree str	9	8	Right	Ord
17	engsc1	Numeric	1	0	I get good mar	{1, disagree str	9	8	Right	Ord
18	parsc1	Numeric	1	0	don't like to be	{1, agree stron	9	8	Right	Ord
19	peersc1	Numeric	1	0	make friends e	{1, disagree str	9	8	Right	Ord
20	mathsc1	Numeric	1	0	among the bes	{1, disagree str	9	8	Right	Ord
21	schsc1	Numeric	1	0	good marks in	{1, disagree str	9	8	Right	Ord
22	self2	Numeric	1	0	would like to b	{1, agree stron	9	8	Right	Ord
23	appsc2	Numeric	1	0	I'm good lookin	{1, disagree str	9	8	Right	Ord

■ **Figure 5.3**
The 'Variable View'.

the item 'school is boring' in our questionnaire. The next column gives us the values that variable can take on. For 'attsc 1', a value of 1 corresponds to 'agree strongly', 2 to 'agree', 3 to 'disagree' and 4 to 'disagree strongly'. This is an example of how we can convert answers to numbers, something we will always have to do if we want to analyse data quantitatively.

The next column gives us our missing value codes. Missing values commonly occur in quantitative research. This can happen because respondents don't fill in a particular question or because they fill it in wrongly. It is good practice to give a code to those missing values. That way, SPSS can recognise that they are missing and exclude them from analyses. Conventionally, values of 9, 99, 999 and so on are used for missing values. Obviously, our missing value code has to be one that is not a code for that variable (so, if we had a scale from 1 to 10, our missing value code would have to be 99 and not 9). The next two columns (number of columns and alignment) are purely concerned with layout. The final column labelled 'measure' gives us the level of measurement for each variable (nominal, ordinal or 'scale', what SPSS calls continuous variables). We will discuss levels of measurement in the next chapter. One thing to watch out for with this is that SPSS will assign a level of measurement to each variable based on its best guess of what type of variable it is. These are often wrong, so it is a good idea to check these and change them where necessary.

Changing variables or their characteristics, or adding a new variable is easy in SPSS. If you wanted to add a new variable, you can simply type the name in the first column of the bottom row. A number of default values (like 'numeric' in the type column) automatically appear. You can change these using either pop-down menus or by typing in, for example, the label for your values. You can change the characteristics of existing variables in the same way.

■ ■ ■ Our dataset

In this book we will use a dataset collected as part of a study of children in Year 5 of primary school. They were around 10–11 years old when this data was collected. Due to grade retention, some may be older.

The aim of the study was to look at the relationship between pupils' achievement at school, their self-concept and their attitudes to school. Data on parental background, gender and some school variables were also collected.

The data were collected by means of a questionnaire given to each child. The researcher personally administered the questionnaire in all cases, usually with the class teacher present.

School achievement was collected from teachers in two subjects (English and maths) and globally (grade point average) and was based on the results of teacher-made tests.

Self-concept was conceptualised as hierarchical and multidimensional. Items were constructed based on the seven-factor Shavelson model (see Chapter 4). Four items were constructed to measure each factor. A global self-esteem measure containing nine items was also used.

▶

School attitudes were measured using ten items looking at students' attitudes to both school in general and their teachers. They were also asked to award marks to their school.

Two items measure parental background. One measures the education level achieved by the child's primary carers. The second variable measures their socio-economic status by classifying primary carers' occupations based on the International Labor Office's ISCO 88 classification. This data was colleted by asking children to give a questionnaire to their parents. Some school data was collected, namely school type and school environmental quality (a number of quality factors measured by the observer during school visits).

The sample was a random sample of 50 schools. Within these schools all pupils in one class in Year 5 were surveyed.

The dataset has been shortened (there were originally more variables) and cleaned for this book. The labels of a few variables were changed to better preserve the anonymity of schools and respondents.

▨ ▨ ▨ Summary

In this chapter we have introduced our statistics package, SPSS. This is the most widely used statistical software package in the social sciences and is quite user-friendly.

The dataset we will be using was based on a survey study of children in Year 5 of primary school. We collected data on their achievement, their attitudes to school, their self-concept and some parental background data.

▨ ▨ ▨ Exercises

1. Open the dataset. Have a look at the variables and see if you can add a new variable.
2. Try and change the value labels of one of the variables.

■ ■ ■ Chapter 6

Univariate statistics

Now we have explored the process of designing quantitative research studies it is time for us to do some data analysis.

■ ■ ■ Introduction

While it may be tempting to start looking at relationships between variables straight away, it is a good idea to look at our individual variables first. We usually need to know how our respondents have replied to particular questions or how many times a teacher has asked a particular question, for example, before we can go and look at relationships with other variables. We might often just want to know how many boys and girls are in our sample. This kind of descriptive information can give us useful information on our variables and our research questions. Because we are looking at individual variables, this type of analysis is called *univariate analysis*. As well as providing important information, univariate analysis can help us to look out for mistakes that may have been made during data input, for example. We can spot some (but obviously not all) errors by seeing whether there are values which are outside of the range of possible values (for example, if we have coded boys as 1 and girls as 2, we wouldn't expect to find any 3s!).

■ ■ ■ Frequency distributions

As mentioned above, the first thing we want to look at are often things like how many people have answered in a certain way or how many respondents belong to different ethnic groups, for example. The best way to do this is by looking at what we call a *frequency distribution* of the variable. This is simply a list of all the values that variable has acquired in the sample (for example, 451 boys and 449 girls). What I would like to know about in our sample data set is how many kids say they think they get good marks in English. Let's have a look at how we can do this in SPSS.

1. Once we have opened the file we will need to go to the button marked 'Analyze' because this is where all are statistical analyses are to be found.

2. When we click that box, a new one pops up. This lists a whole slew of statistical procedures. We want to choose 'Descriptive Statistics' because at this stage we are just going to describe our variable.

3. When we click this, a new box comes up with a new list of choices. We choose 'Frequencies' because that is where we are going to find the frequency tables (see Figure 6.1).

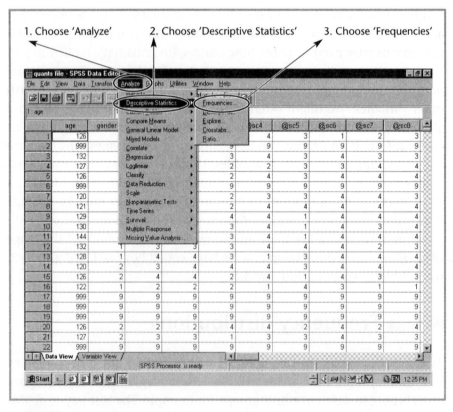

■ **Figure 6.1**
Producing a frequency table: steps 1–3.

4. We now see a box pop up. We will see similar style boxes pop up in most of the analyses we do with SPSS. On the left side within the box we can see a menu giving us the list of all the variables in our data set. In order to do the analyses, we will have to highlight the variable(s) we want to look at (we can put up to 100 variables in the right-hand box at once). We do that by clicking on the variable name, in this case 'engsc 1'.

5. We then need to put that variable in the now empty box on the right. This box needs to contain all the variables we want to include in the analysis. We do this by clicking the arrow in the middle. The variable then jumps to the right-hand box.

6. We click on the button marked 'OK' (see Figure 6.2). (You will have seen that there are a number of other buttons, with names like 'Statistics'. We will look at some of these later on.)

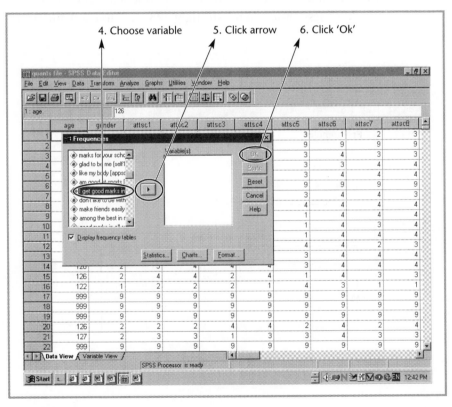

■ **Figure 6.2**
Producing a frequency table: steps 4–6.

Now SPSS will open a new window in which the output will appear. There are two main sections to this output (this will usually be the case in SPSS). The first box gives us some general information: the name of the variable, how many respondents actually answered the question (886) and how many did not (those people coded as missing, 3 in this case) (see Figure 6.3).

The second box gives us our actual frequencies. This box has a number of columns:

1. Column 1 gives us the value labels for the variable we are looking at, in this case 'disagree strongly', 'disagree', 'agree' and 'agree strongly'. As you can see, frequencies will also give us the number of missing values (kids who didn't answer) and the total number of people in the sample.

2. The second column gives us our actual frequencies, the number of kids that have responded 'agree strongly' (237 in this case) and so on.

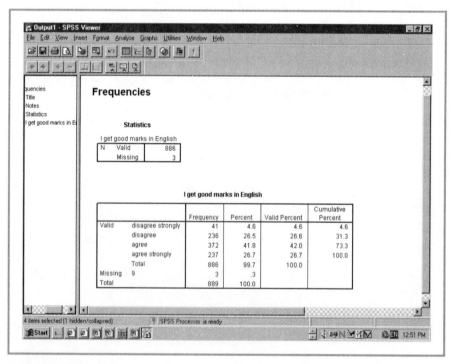

▨ **Figure 6.3**
'Frequencies' output.

3. The third column expresses that as a percentage.

4. The fourth column, labelled 'Valid Percent' gives us the percentage of kids who are not missing (i.e. those that did actually answer the question) for each of the four answer categories.

5. The final column gives us the 'Cumulative Percent'. This just means that the percentages are added up to 100.

This table gives us some interesting information. Promisingly, no values lie outside those that we would expect (the four answer categories and missing). We can also see that the majority of kids (68.7 per cent – we get

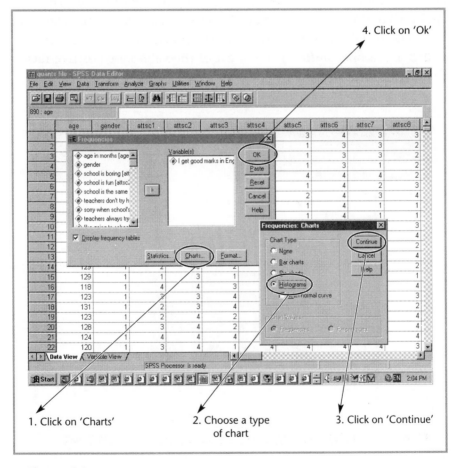

■ **Figure 6.4**

Getting a chart in 'Frequencies'.

this figure by adding the agree and agree strongly totals in the Valid Percent column) think they get good marks in English, but that there is a significant minority who don't think that they get good marks in English. This is obviously a group we might want to single out for particular attention or support.

We can also depict the frequencies in graphical form. To do this, we need to go through steps 1 to 5 in the same way as before, but before we go on to click 'OK', we click on the 'Charts' button. A new pop-up screen will appear which gives us a number of choices, such as pie chart, histogram and bar chart. One of the most useful for us is the bar chart because this will give us a good indication of the distribution of the variable. We can choose this option by ticking the relevant box. Then we click on 'continue'. We then get back to the original frequencies box and click 'OK' (see Figure 6.4). As we can see from Figure 6.5, in this case our variable is *skewed positively*, i.e. most of the values are positive rather than lying in the middle.

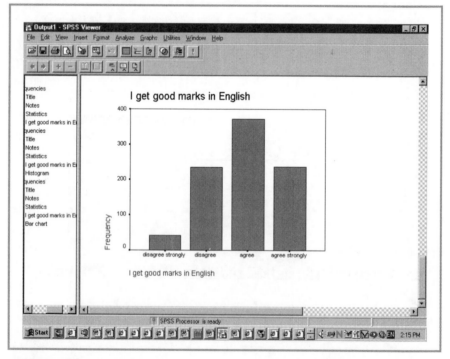

▨ **Figure 6.5**
A bar chart.

Obviously, the frequency table gives us important information about each individual variable. But often we want to be able to 'summarise' our variable using one number that represents the most 'typical' value. This is especially important where we are using variables with a whole load of possible answer categories (think of test scores, for example). To do this, we use a measure of central tendency commonly known as an *average*. In a moment, we are going to look at how we can get SPSS to calculate an average for us. But before we do this, we need to take a look at something called 'levels of measurement'

■ ■ ■ Levels of measurement

Levels of measurement are basically categories of variables. This categorisation is important, because it fundamentally affects the meaning of the variables and what we can do with them statistically, as we will see. There are three basic levels of measurement (some authors distinguish four but for all practical purposes a distinction of three categories is sufficient): *nominal*, *ordinal* and *continuous*.

Nominal variables are measured at the lowest level. These are variables like gender, ethnicity and place of birth, where any numbers we give to the values (e.g. 1 for boys and 2 for girls) only serve to replace a name. The values cannot be placed in order. We can't say 'a girl is more than a boy', for example, so in this case we can't say 2 is more than 1. Nominal variables just have categories which can't be ordered in any way. Any numbers given are merely a descriptor of that category (e.g. 1 = 'boy').

Ordinal variables do possess a natural ordering of categories. An example of an ordinal variable is the one we were looking at earlier, 'I get good marks in English'. Here, a code of 4 was given to 'agree strongly', 3 to 'agree', 2 to 'disagree' and 1 to 'disagree strongly'. These values can clearly be ordered in that someone who 'agrees strongly' 'agrees more' than someone who simply agrees, and so on. This is different from the situation with gender. Therefore, ordinal variables allow you to 'order' the values given. What you can't do is 'measure' exactly the distance between the scale points. Let me explain what I mean by that. When you have a ruler, you know that the distance between 23 and 24 cm is exactly the same as the distance between 10 and 11 cm, i.e. 1 cm. This is not the case when we look at the variable 'I get good marks in English'. Is the distance between 'agree strongly' and 'agree' the same as between 'agree' and 'disagree'? In order to know this, we would have to find out how people thought about these categories, i.e. are these differences the same or different in respondents' minds? And does this differ between different respondents? As we cannot know this, we cannot assume that the distance between each scale point is exactly the same like it is for a ruler. All these 'agree–disagree' type variables are therefore *ordinal*.

Continuous variables are those variables that do behave like a ruler. Not only can we order the categories but also the distance between each scale point is the same. They are measured on a continuous scale, like temperature, weight or height. What variables in educational research are like that? A variable that is often considered to be continuous are scores on a standardised test, such as the SAT. Some authors would argue with that, though, saying that in some cases the distance between scores at the mid point of the scale may not be quite the same as that on the high and low points, but conventionally this type of variable will be considered continuous. We also sometimes want to look at variables like age or birth weight, which are also continuous.

Whether a variable is nominal, ordinal or continuous has important consequences for what type of analyses we can do with it, and how we can interpret the variable, as we will see below.

■ ■ ■ Do ordinal and nominal variables really constitute measurement?

Some researchers say that nominal and ordinal variables are not real measures in the sense that measurement is understood in the natural sciences. They say real measurement means that variables must be continuous and conform to mathematical measurement models. The measurement model that conforms to these requirements is called the Rasch model.

Measures that do not conform to this model are seen as impeding the progress of scientific advancement in the social and behavioural sciences. Obviously, these researchers are not talking about variables such as gender, but about measures of achievement, psychological constructs (e.g. self-concept) and attitudes. These researchers believe that if we were to use the Rasch model to develop our measurement instruments instead of using existing ordinal variables we would be able to improve behavioural sciences to close to what they see as the high level of the natural sciences.

A good overview of these arguments as well as practical applications of the Rasch model is given in Bond, T. G. and Fox, A. (2002) *Applying the Rasch Model.* Mahwah, NJ: Lawrence Erlbaum.

■ ■ ■ Measures of central tendency

The mean, the median and the mode

Now we have discussed levels of measurement, we can have a look at some measures of central tendency or average.

Usually, when we speak about average in every day terms, the value we are thinking of is the *mean*. The mean is simply *the sum of the values of all the cases divided by the total number of cases*. For example, if we had the dataset of the height in cm of people in a class shown in Table 6.1 we would calculate the mean by adding all the heights (= 1,441) and dividing that by the number of people (8), giving us a mean height of 180.125 cm.

Although this is what we commonly mean when we talk about an average in daily life, this type of average actually only works with one type of variable, continuous. Let's think about this. Imagine if we were to take the mean of a nominal variable, let's say gender, which we have also given in Table 6.1. If we calculate the mean gender in the same way, we get a value of 1.44. What does this mean? Is our average person a hermaphrodite with slightly more male than female features? We cannot have such an actual person in our dataset. This value is essentially meaningless. This will be the same for all nominal variables. Imagine if we took birthplace. We could calculate a mean, say 4.6, but would that mean? Someone who came from between Manchester and London but was closer to Manchester? The same problem occurs when we use ordinal variables. The final column in Table 6.1 is an ordinal variable, the answers to a scale asking them whether they liked their job. The mean value is 2.56. But that value does not correspond

■ **Table 6.1** Height, gender and whether respondent likes their job

Case number	Height (cm)	Gender (1 = female, 2 = male)	Likes their job (4 = agrees strongly, 3 = agree, 2 = disagree, 1 = disagree strongly)
1	167	1	1
2	178	1	4
3	189	2	3
4	201	2	3
5	182	1	2
6	175	2	4
7	162	1	1
8	187	2	2
9	180	1	3
Total	1,441		

to any of the answers – it is somewhere between agree and disagree, but a bit closer to agree. This doesn't make too much sense either.

Therefore, we will also want to use other types of measures of central tendency. One of these is the *median*. The median is essentially the middle category of a distribution. We can find that by ordering our values from low to high, and then seeing which one the middle one is.

In Table 6.2 we have ordered heights from low to high. To find the median we have to look at which is the middle value. As we have nine observations, our middle category is number 5, or 180 cm, in this case a value that is very similar to the mean. This type of average is most suitable for ordinal variables because it is based on the principle of ordering that is typical of ordinal variables. Here, for example, when we try the same thing for the 'like my job' variable (have a go at this if you want), we find that the median is 3, a far more sensible value that actually corresponds to a real value ('agree'). This one still doesn't work for the nominal variables, though, as we can't sensibly order those (think about ordering birthplaces).

■ **Table 6.2** Height, gender and whether respondent likes their job
ordered by height

Case number	Height (cm)	Gender (1 = female, 2 = male)	Likes their job (4 = agrees strongly, 3 = agree, 2 = disagree, 1 = disagree strongly)
1	162	1	1
2	167	1	1
3	175	2	4
4	178	1	4
5	180	1	3
6	182	1	2
7	187	2	2
8	189	2	3
9	201	2	3

■ ■ ■ How do we calculate the median if we have an even number of cases?

If we have an even number of cases, then the median will be a hypo-thetical value lying between the two middle cases in the distribution. For example, if we have the following set of data:

2   4   6   8   10   12

Our median would be the value that lies between 6 and 8 (the mean of those two middle values, in fact), i.e. 7.

That is why there is a final type of average, the *mode*. The mode is simply the most common value. In our example of gender above, there are 5 females and 4 males, so the modal value is female.

Does that mean that whenever we have a continuous variable we use the mean, whenever we have an ordinal variable the median and whenever we have a nominal variable the mode? Almost, but it is not quite as simple as that. There is one situation where we might want to use the median for continuous variables as well. Table 6.3 gives the fictional distribution of wages in an organisation.

'Wages' is clearly a continuous variable and therefore the mean would seem to be the sensible method to use if we want to calculate the most typical value or average. The mean here is £73,818 (812,000/11). When we look at this figure though, something slightly peculiar seems to have happened. This mean wage is higher than that of ten out of the eleven employees of this organisation. What is going on here is that one person (let's, for the sake of argument, refer to this individual as the vice-president of the organisation) is earning a whole lot more than anyone else. This is what we call an *outlier*. Because the wages of the vice-president lie so far outside the range of the other values the mean is pulled towards that high value and is no longer really representative. Where such outliers exist it can be better to use the median, even with continuous variables (the median in this case is £32,600, a far more representative value).

▓ **Table 6.3** Wages in an organisation

Observation	Wages (£)
1	27,900
2	38,400
3	20,100
4	26,400
5	60,000
6	42,600
7	22,700
8	55,700
9	550,000
10	25,600
11	32,600
Total	812,000

Calculating measures of central tendency in SPSS

Let's have a look at how we can generate some measures of central tendency in SPSS. When we ask the programme to give us a frequency table, we can also ask it to give us some measures of central tendency as well, so we will start by looking at the frequencies for the variable 'I think I'm good at English'.

We want to start once again with steps 1 to 3 above (go into 'Analyze', choose 'Descriptives statistics', then choose 'Frequencies'). As we know, a box now appears in which we have to select the variable (step 4), and click the arrow (step 5) to add it to the list of variables we are going to analyse. Before pressing 'OK', we can now have a look at one of the other buttons on the bottom of the screen, which is labelled 'Statistics' (see Figure 6.6).

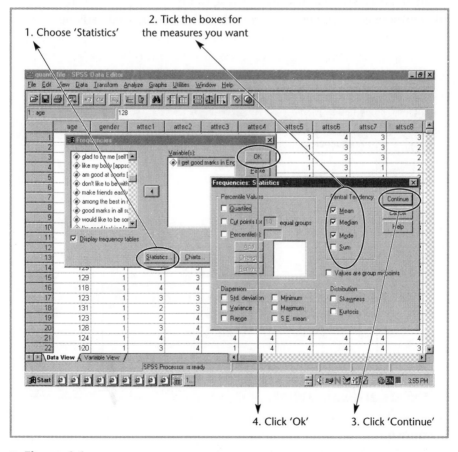

■ **Figure 6.6**
Measures of central tendency in SPSS.

When we press this button, a new screen appears that gives us a number of options. On the right it says 'Central Tendency'. There are a number of measures we can choose. We need to tick the boxes for each measure we want. As you can see, the mode, median and mean are all given as options. Let's tick all three. Once we have done that, we can click 'Continue' and then 'OK' in the main panel, and our output will appear.

We can now see that as well as the output we got last time we used 'Frequencies', we now have a new set of items to look at (see Figure 6.7).

This box gives us our measures of central tendency: the mode, median and mean. We can see here that our mode is 3. This is the value that is most common, in this case the answer than most respondents have chosen (agree). The median is also 3. This is the middle value of the distribution once we have ordered all our answers from lowest to highest. Finally, our mean is 2.91. This values does not actually correspond with any real answers because 'I get good marks in English' is an ordinal variable.

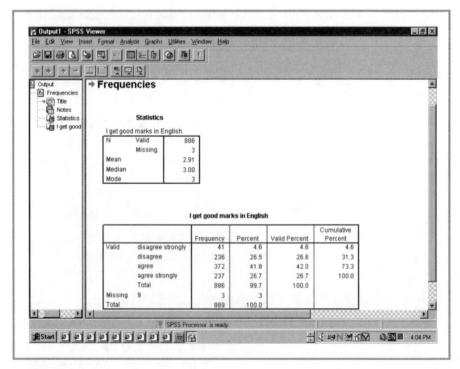

■ **Figure 6.7**
Measures of central tendency output.

■ ■ ■ Measures of spread

Range, interquartile range and standard deviation

Measures of central tendency give us one set of important information when it comes to describing our variables. They don't tell us the whole story, though. Take, for example, the two sets of (fictional) test scores in two schools shown in Table 6.4.

The median and mean score for both schools are equal, at 70. This could lead us to conclude that both have equal patterns of achievement. However, if we look at the data more closely there is clearly more going on than that. While measures of central tendency are the same, they have been arrived at in rather different ways. In school 1, there is quite a spread of values ranging from 45 to 95 , while in school 2 all pupils seem to have scores that are closer together, the lowest being 60 and the highest 80, with six pupils getting 70. If, on the basis of measures of central tendency, we concluded that achievement in both schools is similar, we

■ **Table 6.4** Test scores in two schools

Case no.	School 1	School 2
1	45	60
2	50	65
3	55	65
4	60	70
5	65	70
6	70	70
7	70	70
8	75	70
9	80	70
10	85	75
11	90	75
12	95	80
Mean	70	70
Median	70	70

would be missing out on some important distinctions here. The spreads of the values around the mean or median are clearly different.

That's why, as well as measures of central tendency, we also need measures of spread if we are to give a good description of our variables.

The first way of looking at spread seems obvious: why not just subtract the lowest from the highest scores to give us the *range* of values in our dataset. If we do this with the example in Table 6.4 above this would give us a spread of 50 for school 1 and a spread of 20 for school 2, which captures pretty well the distinction between the two. This measure doesn't always work that well though. Think about our example in Table 6.3, where we looked at wages in an organisation. If we took the range there, subtracting the lowest from the highest value, we would end up with £529,500. This seems like a massive range, suggesting that the values lie spread out a long way away from the mean. When we look at the data more closely though, this is not really the case. Rather, it is once again the one outlier that is distorting this statistic by making the measure of spread seem larger than it should.

What can we do to solve this problem? One common method is to use a measure known as the *interquartile range*. The interquartile range is calculated by first ordering the sample from low to high, and then dividing it into four quarters (see Table 6.5).

We then need to calculate the third and first quartile. The first quartile is given by the first line in Table 6.5. It lies between 55 and 60 in school 1 (we take the mean of those two values, like we did for the median where we have an even number of cases) and is 57.5. In the second school it lies between 65 and 70 (67.5). Then we calculate the third quartile. This is between 80 and 85 in school 1 (82.5), and between 70 and 75 (72.5) in school 2. We then can finally calculate the interquartile range by subtracing the first from the third quartile:

School 1: Q3 – Q1 = 82.5 – 57.5 = 25
School 2: Q3 – Q1 = 72.5 – 67.5 = 5

Again we see that the spread in school 2 is far smaller than in school 1.

This measure is less likely to be distorted by outliers than the range as it cuts out all extreme values at the top and bottom of the distribution. However, a disadvantage of this method is that it only uses a small amount of the information that could be used, as we are only looking at two values when calculating the range. A measure that does use all the

■ **Table 6.5** Calculating the interquartile range

Case no.	School 1	School 2
1	45	60
2	50	65
3	55	65
4	60	70
5	65	70
6	70	70
7	75	70
8	75	70
9	80	70
10	85	75
11	90	75
12	95	80
Mean	70	70
Median	70	70

information we have, because it takes all values into account rather than just two, is the *standard deviation.*

The standard deviation (SD) is a measure of the extent to which the values in a distribution cluster around the mean. It is related to a value called the *variance*, which you might also encounter. In fact, the standard deviation = the square root of the variance. The variance in turn is the sum of the squared deviations of the observations from their mean divided by the number of observations minus 1. You needn't worry too much about that, but what this basically means is that the variance is calculated by looking at the extent to which each observation differs from the mean. The latter implies that the standard deviation (and the variance of course) can only be calculated where we can calculate a mean. Therefore you can only calculate a standard deviation of continuous variables. With ordinal variables it is better to use the range. If we have nominal variables, it does-n't make sense to calculate measures of spread at all.

In Table 6.5, we would find a standard deviation of 14.6 for school 1 and of 4.8 for school 2, which again shows clearly the difference in patterns of responses between the two.

Calculating measures of spread in SPSS

How can we calculate measures of spread using SPSS? Let's look once more at our variable 'I think I am good at English'. Again we don't need to look further than our frequencies we used earlier. We can once more go through steps 1 to 5 ('Analyze', 'Descriptive Statistics', 'Frequencies', select 'Variable(s)', click arrow) and, as with the measures of central tendency, click on the 'Statistics' box (see Figure 6.8). We can then see that in that same box, as well as there being the option to check a number of measures of central tendency, we can also tick boxes for a number of measures of spread. We

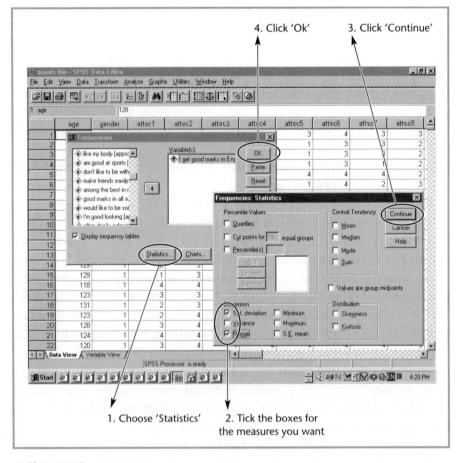

▥ **Figure 6.8**
Measures of spread.

will choose range and standard deviation, and click 'Continue'. Once we
have 'OK'ed in the main box, the output will appear (see Figure 6.9).

If we look at the output, we can see that along with the measures of
central tendency, we now also have a number of measures of spread. The
first measure given in the top box is the standard deviation. This is 0.843.
In a large sample, approximately 68 per cent of respondents will lie one
SD from the mean. We know that the mean was 2.91. Therefore 68 per
cent of observations are likely to lie between 2.91 – 0.843 (= 2.067) and
2.91 + 0.843 (= 3.753), and 95 per cent of observations are likely to lie
within 2 SD of the mean. The problem in this case, though, is that these
values do not correspond with any actual responses that could be part of
this agree strongly–disagree strongly type scale. This is because this is an
ordinal variable. A better measure here is the range. This is 3, which corresponds with the difference between the highest and lowest value.

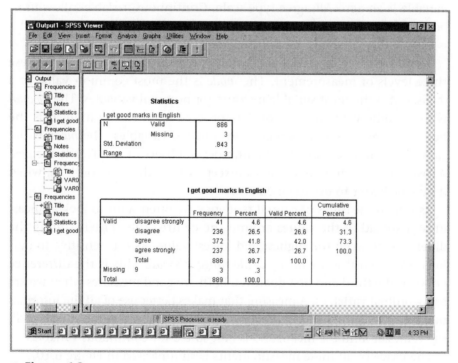

■ **Figure 6.9**
Output measures of spread.

■ ■ ■ Summary

In this chapter we have looked at describing single variables. This is called univariate analysis. One of the most obvious (and most important) things to do at the start of an analysis is to look at the frequency distribution of the variables. As well as looking at the frequency distribution, we will usually want to be able to describe the most typical or average case or response. To do this we calculate measures of central tendency.

In order to be able to do this we need to know at what level our variable is measured. There are three levels of measurement: nominal, ordinal and continuous. Nominal variables, like ethnicity, don't allow us to order categories. Any numbers or categories we assign are just labels. Ordinal variables allow us to order categories from low to high or from less to more (or disagreement to agreement), but we can't measure precisely what the distance is between scale points. A typical ordinal variable is an agree/disagree type scale. Continuous variables allow us to both order categories and to say that the distance between all categories is exactly the same (like measuring length with a tape measure).

There are three measures of central tendency that go along with these three levels of measurement. The *mode* is the most common value in a dataset. It is the most suitable measure for nominal variables. The *median* is the middle value in a set of data ordered from low to high. It is the best measure of central tendency for ordinal variables. The *mean* is the sum of all values divided by the number of observations. This is the best measure for continuous variables (except where there are outliers, when it may be better to use the median).

As well as measures of central tendency we often want to look at measures of spread of the values around the centre. The *range* is simply the difference between the highest and lowest value. As it is sensitive to outliers, we often use the *interquartile range* instead. This is the difference between the third and first quartiles. Both are good measures when we are using ordinal variables. A measure that makes better use of all the information we have is the *standard deviation*. This is a measure of the spread of all the values around the mean, and is best suited for continuous variables.

The usage of all these measurements is summarised in Figure 6.10.

	Central tendency	Spread
Nominal	Mode	–
Ordinal	Median	Range
		Interquartile range
Continuous	Mean	Variance
	Median (if outliers are a problem)	Standard deviation

■ **Figure 6.10**
Describing single variables.

■ ■ ■ **Common misconceptions**

1. *If a variable is measured in numbers, we can order it, can't we?* Not necessarily. When we use statistics, we have to assign numbers to our categories in order to do calculations. In some case, these numbers are merely a replacement for an unorderable label, like place of birth. We could assign a 1 to France, 2 to Spain, 3 to England and so on, but that doesn't mean that we could order them in any way.

2. *Average and mean are the same thing, aren't they?* In daily life, when we talk about average, we are usually referring the mean. In statistics, however, the mean is actually only one possible average. The mode and the median are also averages.

3. *When we have continuous variables, we always use the mean as the measure of central tendency, don't we?* Not necessarily. The mean is not always the best measure of central tendency for continuous variables. Outliers (extreme cases) can distort the mean, as we saw in Table 6.3. When we have such outliers, the median may be a more accurate representation of central tendency.

4. *When we have nominal variables, we use the range as our measure of spread, don't we?* No. When we have nominal variables, the concept of spread is meaningless. As we can't order the categories, the concept of them being spread (around the mode) is not a useful one.

■ ■ ■ Exercises

1. Have a look at the datafile on the website. Can you find an example of a nominal, an ordinal and a continuous variable?

2. Have a look at the frequency distributions for the variables 'I like going to school' and 'school is boring'. What can you say about these two variables?

3. Can you compare the central tendency and spread of the two variables 'I like going to school' and 'school is boring'? Which measures do you use and what do they tell you?

4. Can you compare central tendency for grades in maths and English? What measure do you use? What does this tell you?

5. Can you compare the spread of the variables grades in maths and English. What measures do you use? What do they tell you?

■ ■ ■ Further reading

Any basic statistics text will contain a section on measures of central tendency and spread. For a more mathematical treatment than we have given here, the following text is good: Wonnacott, T. J. and Wonnacott, R. J. (1990) *Introductory Statistics* (Wiley).

Another good introduction is given in Aliaga, M. and Gunderson, B. (2002) *Interactive Statistics* (Sage).

■ ■ ■ Chapter 7

Bivariate analysis: comparing two groups

■ ■ ■ Introduction

Now we have described individual variables (univariate analysis), it is time for us to have a look at the relationship between two variables. This is called *bivariate analysis* and will form the subject of this and the next chapter.

In educational research we often want to look at the relationship between two variables. Do boys do better than girls in reading? Is there a relationship between attendance at school and pupils' self-concept? These and many other questions will necessitate the use of bivariate analyses.

Looking at the relationship between two variables or bivariate analysis involves a number of different statistical methods which are related to the different levels of measurement discussed in Chapter 6. If you remember, we said that there were three main levels of measurement: nominal (the numbers are only labels, we can't order the categories, e.g. gender), ordinal (we can order the categories, but we can't say that the difference between the categories is always exactly the same, e.g. items like 'I think I'm good at school'), and continuous (can be ordered and distance between categories is always the same, e.g. height in cm). What method we can use will depend on the level of measurement of the two variables we are looking at. If you can't quite remember what these different levels of measurement are, have another look at Chapter 6.

An important factor to remember when we are looking at the relationship between two variables is that we will want to look at two things: we want to know whether the relationship is statistically significant (low probability of occurring in the sample if there was no relationship in the population) and how large the effect size (strength of the relationship) is. In some cases the same method will give us information on both these things, but in other cases we are going to need to look at the two separately. Have another look at Chapter 4 if you can't quite remember what significance and effect sizes are.

■ ■ ■ Cross tabulation – looking at the relationship between nominal and ordinal variables

What is cross tabulation?

The first statistical method we will look at is used to compare *two nominal variables, a nominal and an ordinal variable or two ordinal variables (as long as they don't have too many different categories)*. The method is called *cross tabulation*.

The essence of the method is quite simple: a cross tabulation is a table that shows the number of cases falling into each combination of the categories of two or more variables. This may sound a bit complicated, so let's illustrate it with an example. Suppose I have collected some data on the gender and ethnicity of students in my quantitative methods and statistics classes and want to find out whether women and men are differently represented in the different ethnic groups. I can start to do this by counting the number of men and women in each group and collating a cross tabulation table, which would look like Table 7.1.

As we can see, there appear to be more women among the English and Chinese groups, and more men among the Other European group. While this is useful information, it does not necessarily tell us whether or not there is a relationship between the variables gender and ethnicity. To help us do that, we need to calculate the number of cases expected to fall in each cell if there was *no* relationship between the two variables. To do this, we need to know the percentage of either the row (ethnicity) or column (gender) variables of the whole. Let us use the columns (gender). In total, there are 23 men and 31 women. This means that men make up 42.6 per

■ **Table 7.1** Cross tabulation of gender and ethnicity (1)

	Men	Women	Total
White English	10	17	27
Chinese	6	8	14
Other European	7	6	13
Total	23	31	54

cent of the sample ((23/54)*100), and women make up 57.4 per cent of the sample. Knowing this, we can calculate the number of men and women we would expect to find in each ethnic group. If there was no relationship, we would expect that men and women would be represented in each group in the same proportion as we find them in the sample. Or, to put that in a different way, if the number of men and women was unrelated to the ethnic group to which they belong, we would expect the distribution of the genders within each ethnic group to be about the same, and to be the same as in the sample as a whole. Therefore, we would expect about 42.6 per cent of White English, 42.6 per cent of Chinese and 42.6 per cent of Other European students to be men.

This is how we calculate expected values: there are 27 White English students. If there was no relationship between ethnicity and gender, we would expect 42.6 per cent of those 27 (27*0.426) = 11.5 to be men and 57.4 per cent of those 27 to be women (27*0.574 = 15.5). So we would expect there to be 11.5 men and 15.5 women if there was no relationship between gender and ethnicity. We can do the same for the other ethnic groups:

Chinese: 42.7% of 14 = 6 men, and 57.4% of 14 = 8 women

Other European: 42.7% of 13 = 5.5 men and 57.4% of 13 = 7.5 women

If we add those figures to the previous table we get Table 7.2.
If we look at this table, we can see that there are less White English men

■ **Table 7.2** Cross tabulation of gender and ethnicity (2)

	Men	Women	Total
White English			
Actual	10	17	27
Expected	11.5	15.5	27
Chinese			
Actual	6	8	14
Expected	6	8	14
Other European			
Actual	7	6	13
Expected	5.5	7.5	13
Total	23	31	54

and more White English women than we would expect if there were no relationship between the variables. There are more Other European men and less Other European women than we would expect if there were no relationship. Finally, there are exactly the number of men and women we would expect if there were no relationship among the Chinese students.

Doing cross tabulations in SPSS

Let's have a look at how we can produce cross tabulations in SPSS. Let's look at whether girls and boys in our dataset differ on their answer to the question 'I don't like the way I look'. We could hypothesise that they may differ here, as society may place a greater premium on female than on male appearance, leading to lower levels of self-concept in this area among female respondents.

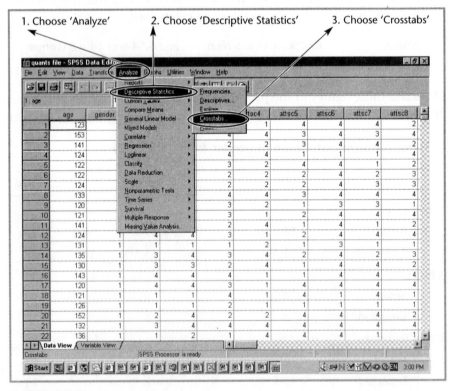

▨ **Figure 7.1**
Producing a cross tabulation table: steps 1–3.

1. As usual, the first thing we need to do is go into 'Analyze'

2. In the pop-up list that appears, we choose 'Descriptive Statistics'.

3. A new pop-up list appears. The fourth item is called 'Crosstabs' (see Figure 7.1). This is the one we want.

A new box pops up. This is the cross tabulations procedure box. Now we have to choose which variables we want to analyse. We want to look at the relationship between gender and 'I don't like the way I look'.

4. We select the variable 'don't like the way I look' from the list on the left.

5. We click on the arrow next to the 'Row(s)' box (see Figure 7.2). The variable is now in the 'Row(s)' box.

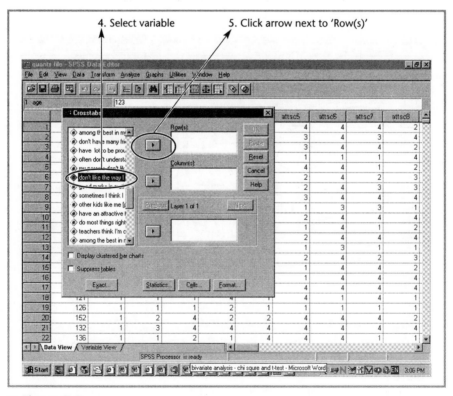

■ **Figure 7.2**
Producing a cross tabulation table: steps 4 and 5.

6. We select the variable 'gender' from the list of variables.

7. We click the arrow next to the 'Column(s)' box. Gender is now in the 'Column(s)' box (see Figure 7.3).

Then we press 'OK'.

The output appears in a new window as usual (see Figure 7.4).

The first box that appears in the output window gives us the number of kids who have given an answer to both questions (885, or 99.6 per cent of respondents), those that have not answered one or both the questions (the missing values, 4 or 0.4 per cent), and finally the total sample size (889).

The actual cross tabulation table is given below that. As you can see, it is very similar to the table we constructed about my students earlier, with the

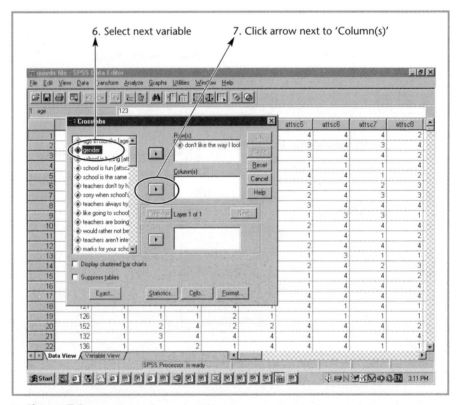

▧ **Figure 7.3**
Producing a cross tabulation table: steps 6 and 7.

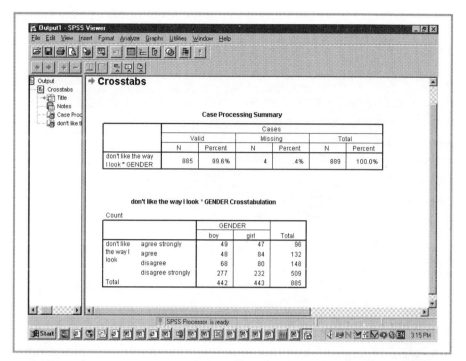

■ **Figure 7.4**
'Crosstabs' output.

columns representing gender, and the rows 'I don't like the way I look'. So, for example, 49 boys agreed strongly that they didn't like the way they looked. The row and column totals are also given.

What is missing here are obviously the expected numbers if there was no relationship between the two variables (i.e. if boys and girls did not differ in their views on how much they like the way they look). SPSS will give us these as well, if we ask it to.

8. To get the expected values, we need to go through steps 1 to 7 as before, but before we click on 'OK', we need to click on the 'Cells' button.

9. A new box appears. We can see that under 'Counts' 'Observed' has already been ticked. Underneath that it says 'Expected'. We need to tick this box.

10. We press 'Continue', and finally 'OK' (see Figure 7.5).

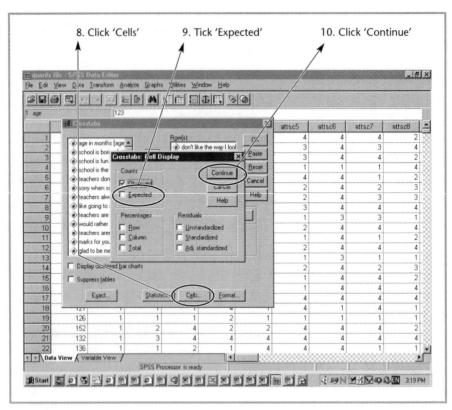

■ **Figure 7.5**
Obtaining expected values in 'Crosstabs': steps 8–10.

We get a new output window (see Figure 7.6). If we look at the cross tabulation table, we can immediately see the change from the previous analysis: instead of just having the actual count in our sample ('count'), we also have the 'expected count' for each cell underneath that. This is the expected number of responses in each cell if there was no relationship between gender and the variable 'I don't like the way I look', and is calculated in the way we outlined in our example above. We can see in the table, for example, that if there was no difference between boys and girls, 254.2 boys and 254.8 girls would be expected to disagree strongly with the statement 'I don't like the way I look'. In actual fact, 277 boys and 232 girls strongly disagreed, so that would suggest that boys are more likely and girls less likely to disagree strongly with this statement than you would expect if there was no difference between them.

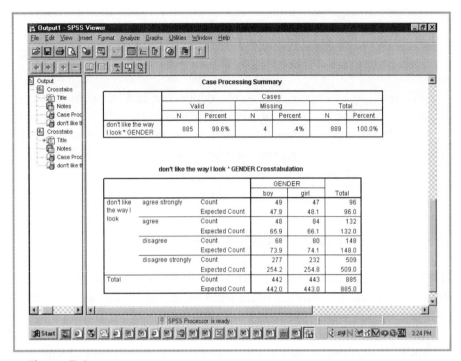

■ **Figure 7.6**
'Crosstabs' output with expected values.

■ ■ ■ How do we know which variable to put in the rows and which in the columns?

As a rule, we will put the independent variable in the columns and the dependent variable in the rows. As we saw in Chapter 1, the dependent variable is our outcome variable, the one we are predicting, or the effect. The independent variable is the predictor or the cause. So, for example, if we were looking at the relationship between gender and body image, gender would be seen as the cause and put in the columns, and body image as the effect (dependent) and put in the rows. (It would not make sense to hypothesise that body image 'caused or predicted' gender!)

In some cases we don't have a hypothesis that can help us determine which variable is dependent and which is independent (e.g. when looking

▶

at the relationship between gender and ethnicity among my students). In that case it does not matter which variable we put in the columns and which in the rows.

Even when we can clearly distinguish dependent and independent variables, one thing to point out is that it makes no difference to the calculation of the cross tabulation which is which. Therefore this is not something you should get too worried about. This is merely a convention, so feel free to break it if you want.

The measure of statistical significance

While we can see that there are some differences between boys and girls in how they respond to this question, what we still don't know is how likely it is that this difference between boys and girls would occur in our sample if there were no difference in the population. As we know, any difference we find in our sample could be the result of chance factors or sampling error rather than a difference in the population (see Chapter 4). That is why we want to calculate the *significance level* or *probability value*, which will tell us how likely it is that we have found a difference this large in our sample if there were no difference in our population.

Usually when calculating significance levels we use *statistical tests*. Throughout this book we will be looking at a lot of statistical tests. They will all basically be looking at the same thing: whether or not our relationship or difference is statistically significant. The first test we will look at is the chi square test. The chi square test tests the hypothesis that the row and column variables are independent or unrelated to one another. It will give us a test statistic, the exact value of which is not important for our purposes, and a significance level or p-value. In order for us to be able to say that the relationship we are studying is statistically significant, the p-value has to be as small as possible. The default value that is usually used to say that a difference or relationship is statistically significant (i.e. that we can be reasonably (but not 100 per cent!) confident that the values we have found are very unlikely to occur if there is no difference in the population) is *less than* 0.05 (this corresponds to a confidence level of 95 per cent). This is obviously an arbitrary cut-off point, and other cut-off points are also used, especially with a large sample, in particular *less than 0.01* (99 per cent confidence level) and *less than 0.01* (99.9 per cent confidence level).

How can we obtain the chi square test and the significance level in SPSS? We start by going through steps 1 to 10 above. But before we go on to click 'OK', we go through another couple of steps:

11. At the bottom of the crosstabs box there is a button marked 'Statistics'. We click this.

12. A new box appears with a number of choices. We tick the box marked 'Chi-square'.

13. We click on 'Continue' and then on 'OK' (see Figure 7.7).

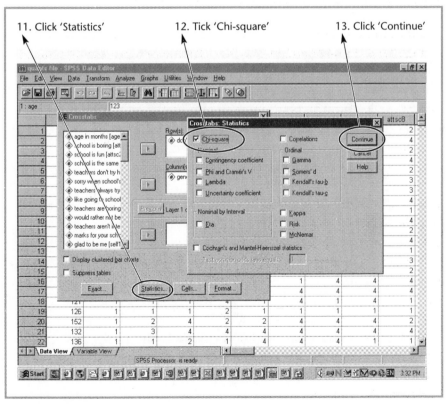

▪ **Figure 7.7**
Obtaining the chi square test in 'Crosstabs': steps 11–13.

When we look at the output (see Figure 7.8), we can see that underneath the cross tabulation table we have a new box with a number of test statistics in it ('Pearson Chi-Square', 'Likelihood Ratio', and 'Linear-by-Linear Association'). This, as will often be the case with SPSS output, is more information than we really need. The one we want to look at is the first one, 'Pearson Chi-Square'. As I mentioned above, we are not that interested in the actual statistics (the first column) and the same goes for the second column (df). The column we want to look at is the third one, labelled 'Asymp. Sig.' (asymptotic significance). This is the p-value. In this case the p-value is 0.002. That means that, using the 0.05 cut-off point, our difference is statistically significant. We will need to include the chi square statistic and df when we write up our results, so other researchers can replicate our findings. We would report our findings a bit like this: 'A significant difference was found in the responses of boys and girls to the item "I don't like the way I look" (chi square = 14.81, df = 3, p = 0.002)'.

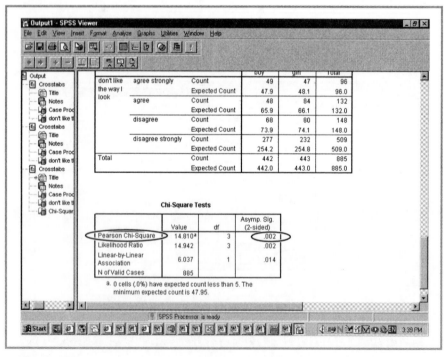

■ **Figure 7.8**
Chi square test output.

What does that tell us? Merely that there is a low probability that the differences we have found are due to chance sample fluctuations. It doesn't tell us where the differences lie (are girls more or less likely than boys to agree to this statement?), or how strong the relationship between the variables 'I don't like the way I look' and 'gender' is.

To answer the first of these questions, we need to have a look at back at the actual cross tabulation and compare the expected and actual values. If we do that, we can see that boys and girls answer 'totally agree' at almost exactly the levels we would expect if there were no relationship between the variables (expected and actual counts are almost the same). The situation is different for the other categories. Girls are more likely to agree that they don't like the way they look (84 actual, as opposed to 66.1 expected if there were no relationship). Girls are also slightly more likely to disagree that they don't like the way they look than expected (80 actual as opposed to 74.1 expected, a small difference), and are less likely to strongly disagree that they don't like the way they look than expected (234 actual, 254.8 expected). Clearly, while there is a significant difference, the relationship is a complex one!

■ ■ ■ Conditions under which we can use the chi square test:

We can only use the chi square test if the following conditions are met:

1. The two variables we are looking at have to be *nominal or ordinal,* not continuous.

2. No cell should have an *expected value of less than one.* We can find this out by looking at the expected values in the cross tabulation table. None of these should be less than one.

3. No more than 20 per cent of the cells should have *expected values less than five.* We can find this out by counting the number of cells with an expected value of less than five in the cross tabulation table (e.g. 10) and seeing what percentage that is of all cells (e.g. 20 cells in total would make 50 per cent so we should not use the chi square test in this example).

The measure of effect size: phi

The other question that the chi square tests did not answer was how strong the relationship is. You might think we could answer this question by looking at the p-value. The more significant, the lower the p-value and therefore the stronger the relationship. This is not correct, however. As we saw in Chapter 4, the significance level is only partly determined by the strength of the relationship. It is equally determined by sample size. Therefore, we need a different measure to look at the strength of the relationship, or the *effect size*.

Regrettably, SPSS doesn't necessarily include measures of strength of relationship. However, they are usually easy to calculate. The effect size for the chi square test, which is called *phi*, is calculated by taking the square root of the calculated value of chi square divided by the overall sample size. In our example this would give us the following results:

1. Chi square can be found in the 'chi squares test', in the column labelled 'value'. We want to use Pearson's chi square, which is 14.810 in our example.

2. The sample size can be found in the first box of the output. We want the valid sample size, excluding all the missing values (those kids that didn't respond to one of the questions). This is 885.

3. We then divide the chi square by the sample size: $14.810/885 = 0.0167$

4. And take the square root of that figure, which is 0.129.

The question is, what does that mean? Is this a large effect or a small effect? The effect size measure varies between 0 (no relationship) and 1 (perfect positive relationship). Therefore, the closer to 1 the stronger the relationship. As a general rule of thumb, the following cut-off points are sometimes proposed:

<0.1 weak
<0.3 modest
<0.5 moderate
<0.8 strong
≥0.8 very strong

In our example the relationship is modest.

■ ■ ■ With what kind of variables can we use cross tabulations and chi square?

These methods are best suited when we are using:

■ two nominal variables;

■ a nominal and an ordinal variable;

■ two ordinal variables.

We have to be careful when using ordinal variables that they don't have too many categories. Otherwise we might run into the problem that too many cells may have less than five expected cases (see above). Also, when you have a large number of cells, the cross tabulation table becomes unwieldy and hard to interpret.

■ ■ ■ The t-test: comparing the means of two groups

Comparing two means

Using cross tabulations, we have been able to look at the relationship between two nominal and/or ordinal variables. This is obviously insufficient for us to interrogate all our data properly. We will in some cases want to compare means of a *dependent variable* between two groups. We might, for example, want to compare the achievement of boys and girls on a reading test. We might also want to look at the effects of an improvement programme, comparing the achievement of pupils who have been part of the programme to those who have not. Obviously when talking about means we are looking at a continuous variable as our dependent variable (see Chapter 5) and when we are talking about comparing two groups we are usually looking at a nominal variable.

Let's have a look at whether girls do better than boys in English. We could do a cross tabulation of gender and achievement but this would be problematic. 'Grades in English' is a continuous variable with a range of scores going from 31 to 100. This would mean that using a cross tabulation table we would have a large number of cells (well over 200!) which would make the cross tabulation table very hard to interpret. Also, a large number of cells would have expected values of less than five, and many have expected values of zero, which means that the conditions for using cross tabulation and chi square aren't met. This is usually the case when we use continuous variables.

Selecting cases

This means that we need to take a different approach. The first thing we can do to compare the means is to look at those means using the *frequencies* procedure we saw in Chapter 6. In order to be able to do that, we will have to first select the boys, and calculate their means, and then do the same for the girls (or the other way round). This is easy to do in SPSS:

1. Click on 'Data'. A pop-up box appears.
2. Click on 'Select Cases'. A new box pops up (see Figure 7.9).

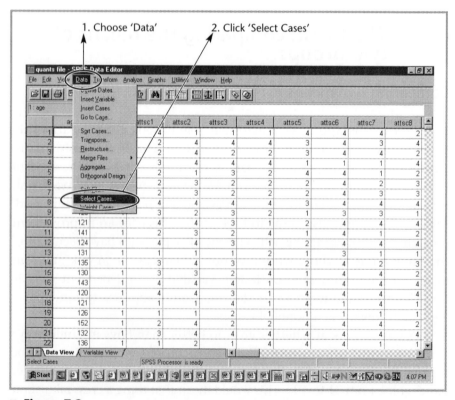

■ **Figure 7.9**
Selecting cases: steps 1 and 2.

3. The default in the 'Select Cases' box is 'All cases'. This means that every respondent is included in the sample. In this case, we only want to look at the boys, so we select the next choice 'If condition is satisfied'.

4. Once we have done this, the button labelled 'If' lights up. We need to click this button because this is where we are going to tell SPSS which cases to select (see Figure 7.10).

5. A new screen appears. First we have to choose the variable we are going to select on, in this case 'gender', and click the arrow. 'Gender' now appears in the box on the right.

6. Now we are going to have to specify what we are going to select. If we look in our file ('Variable View' – see Chapter 1) we can see that boys are coded 1. Underneath the box is a calculator-like keypad. We click on '=' and then on '1'. Both appear in the box.

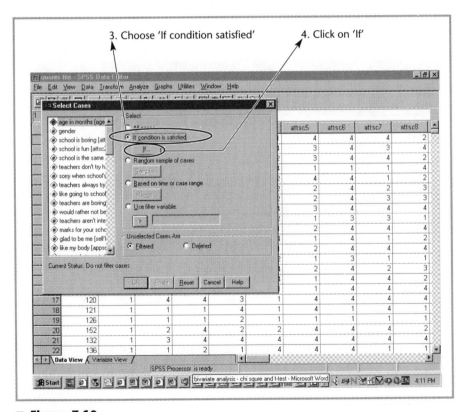

■ **Figure 7.10**
Selecting cases: steps 3 and 4.

7. Now we press 'Continue', and then 'OK' (see Figure 7.11). We have selected only the boys for the analysis.

We can do the same to select the girls (in step 8 replace 1 by 2). To select everyone again, we go through steps 1 and 2, and choose 'Select' 'All Cases' in the screen which appears at step 3.

Once we have selected the boys, any analysis we do will only contain the boys, and the same is true when we select the girls. So we can calculate separate means for both groups using this procedure and the 'Frequencies' procedure we discussed in Chapter 5.

Having done that, we get the following results:

	Boys	Girls
Mean English grades	77.5	79.3

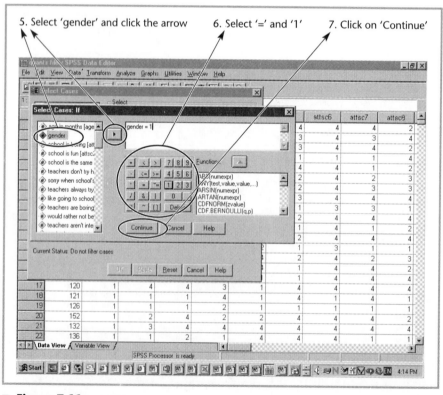

■ **Figure 7.11**
Selecting cases: steps 5–7.

The measure of significance: the t-test

From these results, it looks as though girls do better at English than boys. But, as we have said before, it could be that the difference we have found exists only as a coincidence of our sample rather than resulting from a difference in the population. We need to test whether the difference we have found is statistically significant.

When we looked at nominal and ordinal variables, we used the chi square test to look at significance. This time, when we are looking at the difference between the means of a continuous variable between two groups, we use a different test, called the *t-test*. This test has been designed to test whether the means of two samples differ and can be easily calculated in SPSS. As with chi square, the actual test statistic is not really important to us. What we want to look at is the p-value, or significance level. Once again, the smaller that significance level, the less likely it is that we would have found the difference we have found in our sample if there were no difference in the population. The cut-off point of less than 0.05 also remains the same.

Doing t-tests in SPSS

We will now use SPSS to do a t-test on the difference between girls and boys in English grades. We don't need to look at boys and girls separately, so make sure you are selecting all cases here.

1. As usual, we need to go into 'Analyze' if we want to do any statistical operation on the data.
2. In 'Analyze', we go into 'Compare Means'.
3. And then into 'Independent-Samples T Test'(see Figure 7.12).

The pop-up screen then presents us with a number of choices.

4. We have to choose our dependent variable(s), the variable that we want to predict. In our example, this is 'school grades English'. We can choose as many dependent variables as we like. Select this variable from the list and press the top arrow.

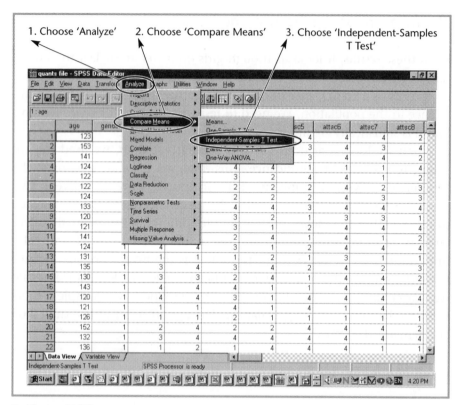

■ **Figure 7.12**
The t-test: steps 1–3.

5. Next, we have to choose our 'Grouping Variable'. This will tell the program which groups we want to compare, in this case boys and girls. Select this variable from the list and press the bottom arrow.

6. Once we have entered the grouping variable, you will see that it is followed by brackets containing question marks. This is because we need to specify how we coded the groups we are going to compare. To do this we need to click the 'Define Groups' box that has lit up (see Figure 7.13).

7. A new box will pop up (see Figure 7.14) and we need to fill in the codes for the two groups we are comparing. In our example we coded boys as 1 and girls as 2, so we need to fill in these numbers.

8. That's the preparation finished, we can press 'Continue' and 'OK' and wait for the results.

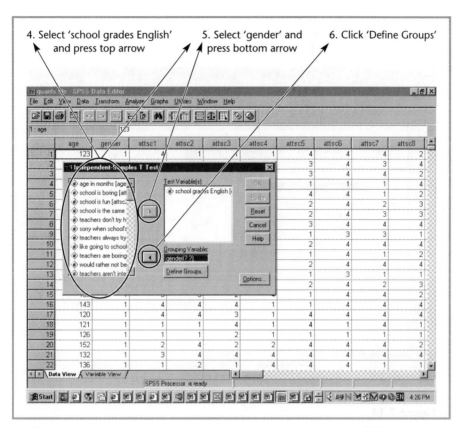

4. Select 'school grades English' and press top arrow

5. Select 'gender' and press bottom arrow

6. Click 'Define Groups'

▨ **Figure 7.13**
The t-test: steps 4–6.

We now have the output screen given in Figure 7.15. But what does it all mean? This is the most confusing output screen we have had so far! Luckily, we won't need all the information supplied. The first box gives us a number of descriptive statistics – the number of respondents, the mean, the standard deviation and the standard error for each group. The results of the t-test can be found in the next box. First off, there are two columns mentioning something called 'Levene's Test for Equality of Variances'. This tests whether the assumption of equal variances between our two groups holds in the data. If variances are (more or less) equal in our dataset, the test should *not* be significant – in this example, the 'Sig.' or significance value is >0.05 (non-significant), so the variance between boys and girls can't be said to differ.

▓ Figure 7.14
The t-test: step 7.

If we look at the next columns, we can see that these are split into two. If variances are equal (Levene's test significance level is *greater* than 0.05), we can use the top row of values. If the variances do differ significantly (Levene's test significance level is *less* than 0.05) we use the bottom row.

The next seven columns give us the data for the actual t-test. Luckily not all the information is that important to us! The information we really need is given in the columns labelled 't', 'df' and 'Sig.'. The value under the 't' column gives us the actual t-test statistic. This in itself does not tell us that much, but we will need to report it when we write up our results so other researchers can replicate what we were doing (along with the next column, labeled 'df'). Our t-value is –2.04, our df is 573. The number we are really looking for is that given under 'Sig.' – this is our significance level. As we saw in Chapter 4, we conventionally use a cut-off point of 0.05 to indicate statistical significance. Therefore, if our significance is *less* than 0.05, we say that we have found a statistically significant difference between programme and

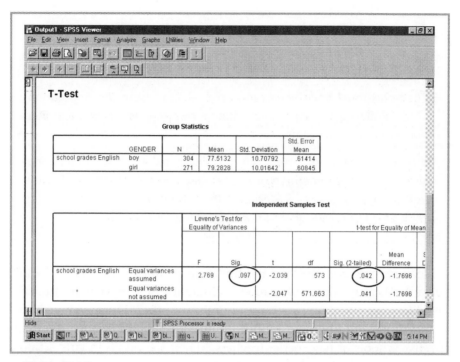

■ Figure 7.15
T-test: output.

comparison schools. In our case, our significance level is 0.042. If we were to write up our results, we would report this something like this: 'Using the t-test for independent samples, we found a significant difference between boys and girls (t = 3.09, df = 576, p<0.05)'.

■ ■ ■ Assumptions that need to be met before we can rely on the t-test

1. The dependent variable must be *continuous*. In Chapter 5, when we discussed measures of central tendency, we said variables needed to be continuous if we are to calculate a mean, therefore, as we are comparing means between groups, our dependent variable has to be continuous here. However, many researchers have used t-tests for ordinal variables (e.g. self-concept, as in dataset 1), and the test is reasonably robust in these circumstances.

▶

> **2.** We can only compare two groups using the t-test. We will see what to do if we want to compare means between more than two groups in Chapter 10.
>
> **3.** Samples must have been randomly selected from the population. This is often a problem in educational research, as samples are often selected for convenience sake.
>
> These conditions are often quite difficult to meet in educational research, and it is something of a relief that research has found that the t-test is quite robust to violations of these assumptions, as long as the samples are large enough and don't differ too much in size.

Meeting these assumptions and finding a significant difference doesn't guarantee that gender really causes a difference in achievement, though. The difference could be caused by a number of other things: some schools in the sample are single-sex schools, so maybe our girls' schools are more effective schools or have better teachers. Maybe the pupils in girls' schools come from higher social class backgrounds or are more able. Unless we have randomly assigned pupils, we will need to control for this kind of factor before we can be confident of our results. In Chapters 9 and 10 we will look at some ways of doing this statistically.

The measure of effect size: Cohen's d

As I mentioned earlier when discussing the chi square test, knowing that the relationship is significant does not tell us whether this effect is strong or weak.

So we need to calculate an effect size as well as the t-test (some would say 'instead of', but that is still a more extreme view). Regrettably, SPSS doesn't yet incorporate effect sizes in all its output (although I'm sure this will soon change!). Luckily, calculating effect sizes is quite easy. There are a wide variety of effect size measures around but the one we will use in conjunction with the t-test is called *Cohen's d*. The formula for this effect size is as follows:

d = (Mean for group A – Mean for group B) / Pooled standard deviation

Where the Pooled standard deviation = (Standard deviation of group 1 + Standard deviation of group 2) / 2.

All this information can easily be found in the SPSS t-test output (box 1). As we saw earlier, the mean for our group A, the boys, is 77.5. The mean for our group B, the girls, is 79.3. The standard deviations are 10.7 and 10.0 for boys and girls respectively. This information can be found in the first box of the output ('Group Statistics'). The formula then becomes:

Pooled standard deviation = (10.7 + 10.0) / 2 = 10.35

D = (79.3 – 77.5) / 10.35 = 0.17

As you can see, this is quite a simple formula that those of you who use spreadsheets could easily incorporate. There are now also some websites that allow you to calculate Cohen's d by filling in the number, such as http://www.uccs.edu/~lbecker/psy590/escalc3.htm.

So, our effect size is 0.17. Does that mean that there is a strong or a weak relationship between gender and achievement in English in our sample?

■ ■ ■ Common misconceptions

1. *When I do a t-test, there are two significance levels. Which do I choose?* In Figure 7.15 you can see that the t-test output screen produces two columns with a significance level (headed 'Sig.'). As we saw earlier, the first of these (column 2) is the significance level for Levene's test of homogeneity of variance. The second (column 5) is the significance level for the actual t-test, which tells us whether the difference between the means is significant.

2. *I've done a cross tabulation and my actual values differ from my expected values. That means there is a relationship between the two variables, doesn't it?* Not necessarily. Any difference could be caused by coincidence, sampling error or measurement error and may not exist in the population. In order to be more confident that the difference is large enough to be very unlikely if it did not exist in the population, we need to use a significance test (chi square).

3. *Does the significance level have to be higher or lower than 0.05?* In order for us to be confident that the difference between the two groups in our sample is the result of differences in the population rather than just a difference in the sample caused by coincidence or

▶

lack of representativeness, it has to be as low as possible. Conventionally, we say that a difference is statistically significant if it is **less** than 0.05.

4. *My significance level is less than 0.05. That means that I can say there is a real difference in the population, right?* Not necessarily! All the assumptions mentioned earlier need to be met before we can say that this is the case.

5. *My significance level is less than 0.05 and I've met all the assumptions. That means that I can say there is a real difference in the population, right?* Not necessarily. Remember that if our significance is 0.05, this means that we still have 5 per cent chance of having drawn a sample in which there is a difference by coincidence that doesn't exist in the population (see Chapter 4).

6. *Where can I find the effect size in SPSS?* At the moment, SPSS does not calculate effect sizes. You will have to calculate the effect size yourself using the formula given above or the website address given.

7. *I have developed a programme to improve reading instruction and used a t-test to compare the results of my pupils to a comparison group. If I have found a significance level of 0.01, and another programme to improve reading has found a significance level of 0.045, that means that my programme works better, doesn't it?* Not necessarily. The significance level can be influenced by a number of factors, like sample size (see Chapter 4). That means that if I had a larger sample than my competitor, my programme will seem to be more significant. That is why we need to use effect size measures.

8. *Students doing my reading programme score significantly better than those that don't. I have a moderate effect size. This means that my programme works, doesn't it.* Sorry to be repetitive, but not necessarily. Unless we have developed a real experiment using random assignment (very rare in education, as mentioned in Chapter 2), our two groups may differ on other aspects than whether or not they have taken part in the programme. The pupils may have higher ability, the teachers may be more effective, etc. We need to do further analyses taking these factors into account (see later) if we are to be certain of this. Also, don't forget the Hawthorne effect we discussed in Chapter 2!

There are some guidelines for determining whether our effect size is strong. Cohen suggests the following:

0–0.20 = weak effect

0.21–0.50 = modest effect

0.51–1.00 = moderate effect

>1.00 = strong effect

While these guidelines can be useful, we do need to be careful not to mechanically follow them, as the cut-off points are again arbitrary and we could start to make exactly the same mistake as effect size supporters have accused the significance test of making!

■ ■ ■ Summary

In this chapter we have started to look at bivariate analysis where we study the relationship between two variables. We have seen that the method we use depends strongly on the measurement level of the variables: are they nominal, ordinal or continuous?

When we have two nominal, a nominal and an ordinal (with a limited number of categories) or two ordinal variables (with a limited number of categories) we can use cross tabulation tables, chi square tests and the phi measure of effect size. Cross tabulation allows us to compare the actual responses in our sample to what we would expect to find if there were no relationship between the data. The chi square test allows us to see whether or not the relationship is statistically significant and the effect size measure allows us to look at how strong the relationship is.

When we want to compare the means on a continuous variable between two groups, we can use the t-test and Cohen's d. The t-test gives us statistical significance while Cohen's d is a measure of effect size.

In both cases we need to take account of the assumptions that need to be met. Figure 7.16 gives us a summary of what we know about bivariate data so far.

		Independent		
		Nominal	*Ordinal*	*Continuous*
Dependent	*Nominal*	Cross tabulation + Chi square + Phi	Cross tabulation + Chi square + Phi	
	Ordinal	Cross tabulation + Chi square + Phi	Cross tabulation + Chi square + Phi	
	Continuous	T-test (2 groups) + Cohen's D		

■ **Figure 7.16**
Summary of bivariate data.

■ ■ ■ Exercises

1. Open the data set. Can you use a test to see whether girls do better than boys at maths?

2. How strong is the difference between the two groups' maths achievement?

3. Can you compare boys and girls on the item 'school is always boring' using the t-test? Explain.

4. Can you compare boys and girls on the item 'school is always boring' using the chi square test? Explain.

5. How strong is the difference between the two groups on this item?

6. Do you think it would be a good idea to stop using the chi square test and the t-test altogether and use effect size indices instead? Explain.

■ ■ ■ Further reading

If you want to find out more about the t-test and chi square test, most statistics textbooks will give you a full mathematical explanation. A good example is Wonnacott, T.J. and Wonnacott, R.J. (1990) *Introductory Statistics* (Wiley), but any statistics textbook will include a section on the t-test and chi square test. The SPSS help files give a clear explanation as well.

Effect sizes have been widely discussed recently. The 'classic' is Jacob Cohen (1988) *Statistical Power Analysis for the Social Sciences* (Lawrence Erlbaum – still in print). This is quite a technical review and not an easy read, however.

More user-friendly overviews of effect sizes can be found in a number of articles, such as Kirk, R. (1996) 'Practical significance: a concept whose time has come', *Educational and Psychological Measurement*, 56, 746–59 and Olejnik, S. and Algina, J. (2000) 'Measures of effect size for comparative studies: applications, interpretations, and limitations', *Contemporary Educational Psychology*, 25, 241–86.

■ ■ ■ Chapter 8

Bivariate analysis: looking at the relationship between two variables

In Chapter 6 we looked at the relationship between two nominal variables, an ordinal and a nominal variable and two ordinal variables with few categories. We also know what to do when we want to look at the difference between the means of two groups.

What do we do when we have two continuous variables, or a continuous and an ordinal variable? This will obviously be a common situation in educational research and is what we will be studying in this chapter.

■ ■ ■ The relationship between two continuous variables: Pearson's r correlation coefficient

What is Pearson's r?

As I mentioned in Chapter 6, continuous variables have some very desirable statistical properties. Obviously, that being the case, we should try to measure our concepts using continuous variables whenever that is possible (although this is more easily said than done in many cases). The method we will use to analyse the relationship between two continuous variables is called the *correlation coefficient*. Basically what a correlation coefficient (there are more than one, as we will see) does is look at whether or not a high score on one variable is associated with a high score on the other. So, if we were to look at two continuous variables in our dataset, grades in English and grades in maths, we would be looking at whether or not a high grade in English would usually go together with a high grade in maths.

As mentioned above, there are actually many different correlation coefficients. Which one to use will depend on what kind of variables we have. When we are working with two continuous variables, we use a correlation coefficient called *Pearson's r.*

What does Pearson's r do? The formula for Pearson's correlation coefficient is given below. (If you want to skip this bit you will be able to follow the rest of the chapter without it but the formula does give some insight into how Pearson's r works, which could deepen your understanding of this method and is why I have included it here.)

If we have two variables, X and Y, the correlation is computed as:

$$r = \frac{\sum_{i-1}^{n} (X_i - \bar{X})(Y_i - \bar{Y})}{(n - 1)S_x S_y}$$

where:

- X_i and Y_i are individual observations (e.g. the grade of a child in English (X_i) and the grade of the same child in maths (Y_i));
- $\bar{X}$ and $\bar{Y}$ are the means for variables X and Y (e.g. the mean grades in English and maths);
- n is the number of cases; and
- S_x and S_y are the standard deviations of the two variables (English and maths) respectively.

So what is actually happening is that the difference between the individual response and the mean for each variable is calculated. These are then multiplied for each individual case. This will give us a positive score if both are positive, so if the respondent scores above the mean on both variables the outcome will be positive. The same is true if the score on both is negative. If the respondent scores below the mean on both variables, the outcome will also be positive. If the respondent has a positive score on variable X and a negative score on variable Y, the outcome will be negative. All these individual scores are then summed to get a total, which is then divided by the product of the standard deviations of both variables to scale it. This will give us the Pearson r correlation coefficient.

Pearson r coefficients vary between −1 and +1, with +1 indicating a perfect positive relationship (a high score on variable X = a high score on variable Y), −1 a perfect negative relationship (a high score on X = a low score on Y), and 0 = no relationship. Thus in our example a correlation coefficient close to 1 would mean that if we scored high in English, we are likely to score high in maths as well. A coefficient close to −1 would suggest that if we scored high in English, we would score low in maths, while a coefficient close to 0 would suggest that getting good grades in English did not predict grades in maths at all (the two are unrelated).

All this means that Pearson's r gives us information about a number of aspects of the relationship:

■ the *direction* of the relationship: a positive sign indicates a positive direction (high scores on X means high scores on Y), a negative sign a negative direction (high score on X means low scores on Y);

■ the *strength* of the relationship: the closer to 1 (+ or −) the stronger the relationship.

Another piece of information we need is whether or not the relationship is statistically significant (unlikely to exist in the sample if it doesn't exist in the population). Once again we have to use a statistical test to find this out. The test we use is called the *F-test*. When we combine the information about the strength of the relationship with information on the size of the sample, we can calculate the F-test along with a p-value which tells us whether or not the relationship is significant. SPSS gives us the p-value along with the correlation coefficient. Therefore we also have information on:

■ the statistical significance of the relationship.

This means that, in contrast to the situation with the chi square and t-tests, we don't have to separately calculate measures of significance and effect sizes (the strength of the relationship).

The p-value for the F-test works in exactly the same way as it did for the other statistical tests: the smaller the p-value the lower the probability that we would have found a relationship in our sample if there was none in the population. The standard cut-off point of <0.05 (or I in some cases <0.01 or <0.001) is used here as well. As for the strength of the relationship, the closer to +/–1 the stronger, the closer to 0 the weaker. Some rules of thumb on effect size are:

<0.+/–1 weak
<0.+/–3 modest
<0.+/–5 moderate
<0.+/–8 strong
≥=+/–0.8 very strong

As you can see, these are the same as when we use the chi square test (see Chapter 7). Once again, I do have to caution you over the use of cut-off points: they are arbitrary, and it is obviously a bit nonsensical to say that a correlation of 0.29 is weak, and one of 0.30 modest!

One thing we need to take into account as well is that the correlation coefficient itself does not tell us how much of the variance in Y is explained by X. For example, if I wanted to know how much of the variance in grades in English is explained by pupils' IQ, we would be able to calculate a correlation coefficient between a measure of IQ and an English language test, but if we wanted to know how much of the variance in English test scores between pupils is explained by differences in their IQ scores, we would have to square the correlation coefficient. So, for example, if we found a correlation coefficient between IQ test scores and grades in English of 0.5, the amount of variance in English test scores explained by IQ scores would be $0.5^2 = 0.25$.

Whenever we are looking at the correlation between two variables, we have to remember that the relationship might be (partly) caused by an underlying factor. For example, in this case it could be that both scores on an IQ test and scores on an English test are partly determined by the pupils' social background. In the next chapter we will look at some ways of taking this into account.

■ ■ ■ Limitations of the correlation coefficient

1. Remember, the fact that two variables are related to one another does not mean that one causes the other. In order to be able to demonstrate that X causes Y, we would also, at a minimum, need to demonstrate that X comes before Y in time, and that there is not a third variable that is causing the relationship (see the example in Chapter 3).

2. The Pearson's r correlation coefficient assumes *linear* relationships, that is relationships where higher scores on X are linearly related to higher scores on Y:

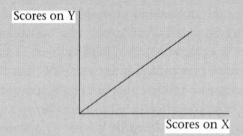

Obviously, not all relationships follow this form. There are curvilinear relationships, for example:

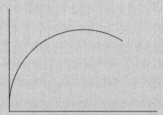

In this case, we have a relationship that is stronger at the start (steep curve), then becomes weaker (less steep curve), and finally zero. An example of this could be the relationship between weeks spent doing a course on correlations and knowledge of correlation. Initially, during the first few weeks, one might see a strong impact on knowledge, but this effect tails off after a while, the effect becoming weaker and eventually becoming 0 as you have nothing further to learn about this subject.

Pearson's r will not be able to tell whether or not the relationship is curvilinear. There are statistical methods that can be used to help overcome this problem, but they are complex and go beyond the confines of this introductory text (see further reading list for information on where you can find out more).

3. Another problem is called *restriction of range*. This occurs when one (or both) of the variables you are measuring has a small range of possible values. When this happens, your correlation coefficient will be artificially low. An example of this can be found in the English education system. It is often said that scores on the end-of-secondary-education assessment (A-level grades) do not predict university course grades well, as the correlation between the two is quite low. This conclusion is not necessarily correct, however. The range of A-level grades that usually give access to university is A to C, and the range of university grades is 1, 2.1, 2.2 and 3, with most clustering around 2.1 and 2.2. This restricted range (rather than poor prediction) is one reason for the low correlations found (another is low reliability of especially university grading).

4. A final issue with the correlation coefficient is that it can be affected by what we call 'outliers'. Outliers are unusual cases. For example, imagine if we had wanted to look at the relationship between spelling and reading test scores among 20 pupils in my class. For 18 of those pupils there is a positive relationship between the two, i.e. those getting high scores in reading also get high scores in spelling. However, two pupils have achieved very high scores in reading and very low ones in spelling. This could have the effect (think of the formula given above) that what is in general a positive correlation would become artificially low or even disappear. Therefore outliers can cause problems, especially in small samples.

How can we calculate Pearson's r in SPSS?

Let's see how we can use SPSS to calculate Pearson's r. We will look at the relationship between English and maths grades, both continuous variables (percentages).

1. As usual, we first need to go into 'Analyze'.
2. In the pop-down menu, we choose 'Correlate'. A new pop-down menu appears.
3. We choose 'Bivariate' (as we are looking at the relationship between two variables) (see Figure 8.1).

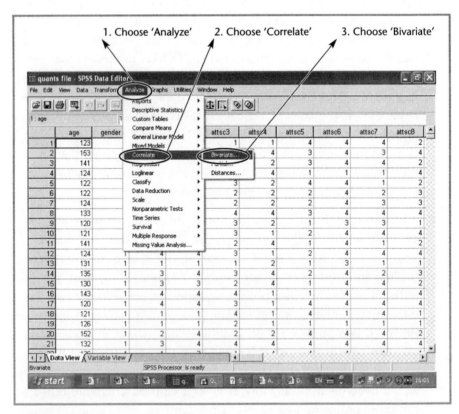

▧ **Figure 8.1**
Correlations: step 1–3.

4. A new box labelled 'Bivariate Correlations' now appears. This is the correlations box. We need to select the variables we want to correlate from the list on the left. We choose 'school grades English' and click on the arrow, and then 'school grades maths' and click on the arrow again. Both now appear in the right-hand box (see Figure 8.2).

5. We click 'OK', and SPSS will calculate Pearson's r for us. (Note that we can put more than two variables in the box, and can calculate correlations for up to 100 variables at once.)

The SPSS output now appears (see Figure 8.3). Correlations are presented in a symmetric table, so all the variables (in this case two) that we are

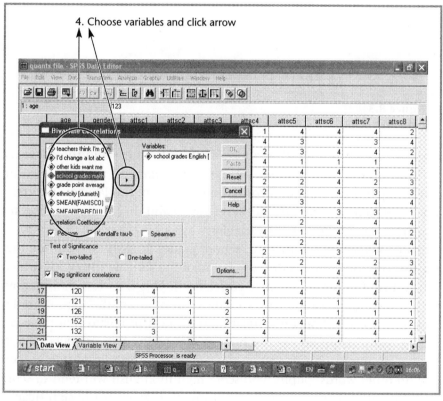

■ **Figure 8.2**
Correlations: step 4.

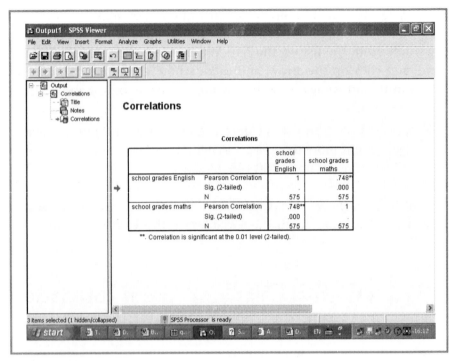

▨ **Figure 8.3**
Pearson's r output.

correlating with one another appear both in the rows and the columns, and we can look across to see all the correlations we are interested in. Three important pieces of information are given: the Pearson r correlation coefficient, the significance level ('Sig.') and the number of cases for which we have data on both variables.

If we look across the row for 'school grades English', we can see that the first column contains the correlation of the variable with itself, which is of course 1 (a perfect positive correlation). This is useless information. In the next column we can see the correlation with 'school grades maths'. The actual Pearson correlation is 0.748. This means that there is a strong relationship between school grades in the two subjects, and as there is no minus sign preceding the coefficient, the relationship is positive. In other words, pupils who score high in English will tend to score high in maths. The next piece of information given is the significance level or p-value. Low values indicate a low probability of us finding a relationship between these two variables in our sample if there was none in the population. Here, the significance level is given as 0.000. This does not mean that the significance level is exactly zero (no p-value is – we never have 100 per cent certainty), but it does indicate a very small value, smaller than 0.001, and well below the 0.05 cut-off value. Finally, we have the N, the number of cases for which we have information on both variables. As you can see, this is 575, so there are quite a number of pupils in the total sample of 889 about who we haven't got this information (we could clearly have done a better data collection job here!). You will also have noted that there are two asterisks after the correlation coefficient. This is because, by default, SPSS flags up any coefficient that is significant at the 0.01 level (this is another of those arbitrary cut-off points we mentioned earlier). We can turn off this option by unticking the 'Flag significant correlations' box following step 4 above.

▓ ▓ ▓ Spearman's rho rank-order correlation coefficient: the relationship between two ordinal variables

What is Spearman's rho

OK, so now we know how to correlate two continuous variables. But what about two ordinal variables? Sometimes we can use a chi square test (if there aren't too many categories, or too many empty expected values below five). We can, however, also use a correlation coefficient.

Can we use Pearson's r? If we look at the formula given above, we can see that Pearson's r calculates the correlation in part by looking at the deviance (difference) between the individual cases and the mean for the variable as a whole. As we saw in Chapter 6, it is not realistic to calculate a mean for ordinal variables (as they can be ordered but we don't know whether the distance between the categories is the same at every scale point). So we won't be able to use Pearson's r as the measure of correlation for two ordinal variables.

What we can do instead, though, is take advantage of the property we know ordinal variables do have: the fact that they are ordered. One measure that is based on this property is *Spearman's rho*.

Basically, what Spearman's rho does is calculate a correlation coefficient on rankings rather than on the actual data. I'll give you an example of what that means: say we have two variables, X (answers to the questionnaire item 'I like doing statistics' on a seven-point scale) and Y (answers to the questionnaire item 'I think I'm good at maths', also on a seven-point scale). Eight respondents have answered these items. This gives us the actual responses shown in Table 8.1.

Table 8.1 Actual responses

Respondent	X (I like doing statistics)	Y (I think I'm good at maths)
1	7	6
2	5	5
3	2	4
4	4	3
5	3	1

In order to calculate Spearman's rho, these actual values are changed into a ranking, as shown in Table 8.2.

Table 8.2 Ranking of actual responses

Respondent number	X (I like doing statistics)	Y (I think I'm good at maths)
1	1	1
2	2	2
3	5	3
4	3	4
5	4	5

A correlation is then calculated on these values, using the following formula:

$$rho = 1 - [(6 * SUM(d^2) / n(n^2 - 1)]$$

where d = the difference in ranks and n is the sample size.

As you can see, what is actual going on here is that we calculate the difference in rank for each individual (e.g. for respondent 3 above, 5 – 3 = 2, for respondent 1, $1 - 1 = 0$), square this (e.g. 3^2), sum all these differences, multiply by 6, and divide by a number that controls for the sample size ($n(n^2 - 1)$). This is then subtracted from 1. So the smaller the numerator (the difference between rankings on the two variables), the larger the correlation. Thus if all ranks were the same and d was therefore to be 0, we would end up with $1 - 0$, or a perfect positive correlation (Spearman's rho = 0).

You may wonder what happens if in our example above two respondents had given the same answer (e.g. 3 on the scale). Their ranking would then be tied. In that case both will be assigned their mean rank.

The interpretation of Spearman's rho is very similar to that of Pearson's r: like Pearson's r, Spearman's rho will vary between -1 and $+1$, with -1 being a perfect negative correlation (if you rank high on X, you will rank low on Y), $+1$ being a perfect positive correlation (if you rank high on X, you will rank high on Y) and 0 being no relationship between the two (rank on X tells us nothing about rank on Y).

As we could for Pearson's r, we can calculate a p-value or significance level for the Spearman's rho rank order correlation using the F-test mentioned above. The interpretation of that is the same as in all the cases we have seen, the lower the p-value, the lower the probability of us finding a relationship in our sample given the hypothesis that there is no relationship in the population.

How to calculate Spearman's rho in SPSS

Calculating Spearman's rho in SPSS is very easy once we know how to calculate Pearson's r. We have plenty of ordinal variables in our sample, so we will choose two for our example: 'I get good marks in maths' and 'I would rather not be at school'.

What we need to do is essentially exactly the same as when calculating Pearson's r. We go through steps 1 to 3 above and select our variables ('I get good marks in maths' and 'I would rather not be at school') in step 4 in the same way as we did when calculating Pearson's r. One thing differs:

5. In the 'Bivariate Correlations' box, we can see that under 'Correlation Coefficients' 'Pearson' is ticked by default. When we want Spearman's rho instead, we simply tick the box marked 'Spearman' and untick 'Pearson' (see Figure 8.4).

6. We then click on 'OK'.

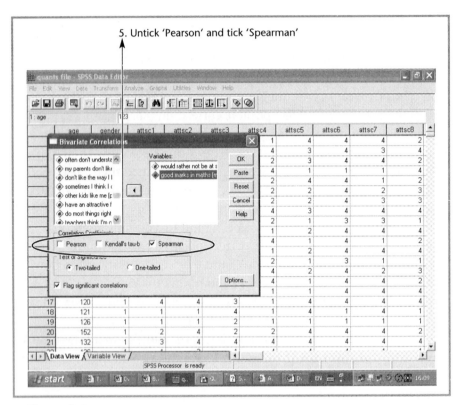

Figure 8.4

Spearman's correlation: step 5.

The output that appears is again almost the same as for Pearson's r (see Figure 8.5). The output is presented in a symmetrical table and gives us information on the correlation coefficient, significance level (p-value) and sample size. If we look across the row for 'I get good marks in maths', we again first see the correlation of the variable with itself and then the correlation with 'I would rather not be at school'. As we can see, the Spearman rank order correlation coefficient is 0.16, a modest positive relationship. The significance level, given as 0.000, tells us that the relationship, though modest in strength, is highly significant (this is because we have a large sample). Finally, the sample size is given as 883.

You will have noticed that as well as Pearson and Spearman, the options under 'Correlation Coefficients' in the 'Bivariate Correlations' box also includes Kendall. This is another rank order correlation coefficient (called Kendall's tau-b) that can be used with ordinal variables. Which one you choose does not really matter (both are calculated

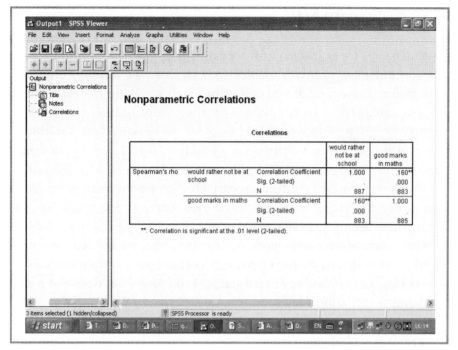

■ **Figure 8.5**
Output of Spearman's rho.

slightly differently but in equally valid ways), although Spearman's rho usually produces higher correlation coefficients than Kendall's tau-b.

Caveats involved with Spearman's rho are similar to those discussed in connection with Pearson's r, although rank order correlations are less influenced by lack of linearity.

■ ■ ■ What do we do if we have one ordinal and one continuous variable?

If we want to look at the relationship between an ordinal and a continuous variable, we need to use a rank order correlation coefficient like Spearman's rho. This is because while variables measured at the higher level (in this case continuous) possess all the characteristics of variables measured at the lower level (in this case ordinal), the inverse is not the case. For example, a continuous variable possesses the attributes of both order and equal distances, while an ordinal variable only possesses the attribute of order.

■ ■ ■ Summary

In this chapter we examined how we can look at the relationship between two continuous or ordinal variables. In both cases, we can use correlation coefficients. These look at whether or not high scores (in the case of continuous variables) or high rankings (in the case of ordinal variables) on variable X go together with high scores or rankings on variable Y. Correlation coefficients vary between –1 and +1. –1 indicates a perfect negative relationship, +1 a perfect positive relationship and 0 no relationship.

Where we have two continuous variables we use the Pearson's r correlation coefficient; where we have two ordinal variables we use Spearman's rho (or Kendall's tau-b).

While correlation coefficients are highly useful, we do need to take a number of restrictions into account: correlation coefficients can be affected by outliers and restricted range, and correlation does not necessarily imply causation.

Figure 8.6 summarises what we have seen about bivariate relationships in the last two chapters.

		Independent		
		Nominal	*Ordinal*	*Continuous*
	Nominal	Cross tabulation + Chi square + Phi	Cross tabulation + Chi square + Phi	Two nominal groups: t-test
Dependent	*Ordinal*	Cross tabulation + Chi square + Phi	Cross tabulation + Chi square + Phi or Spearman's rho	Spearman's rho
	Continuous	T-test (2 groups) + Cohen's D	Spearman's rho	Pearson's r

■ **Figure 8.6**
Summary of bivariate relationships.

Common misconceptions

1. *I have found a significant positive relationship between self-concept and achievement. That means I can say that low self-concept causes low achievement, right?* I'm afraid not. In order to be able to conclude that there is a causal relationship between two variables, three pre-conditions need to be met: (1) there is a relationship; (2) variable X (self-concept) precedes variable Y (achievement) in time; and (3) the relationship is not caused by an underlying variable. Correlation only tells you something about condition 1.

2. *I have a correlation coefficient of 0.35 between a parental socio-economic status index and maths test scores. That means that parental SES explains 35 per cent of the variance in maths test scores, doesn't it?* No, you need to square the correlation coefficient to get an indication of this, so in this case $0.35^2 = 0.12$, or 12 per cent. You also need to take into account that the relationship may become smaller or larger if we include the effect of other variables.

3. *The correlation coefficient is a measure of the significance of the relationship, isn't it?* No, the correlation coefficient is a measure of the strength of the relationship and its direction. The significance is calculated separately using a statistical test that gives us the p-value. The SPSS output gives us both the coefficient and the p-value.

■ ■ ■ Exercises

1. You want to look at the relationship between pupils' responses to the item 'I think I'm good at maths' and their grades in maths. Which method do you use and why?

2. Open the dataset. Is there a relationship between pupils' responses to the items 'I get good marks in maths' and 'I don't like the way I look'? How strong is the relationship?

3. If there is a relationship between pupils' responses to the items 'I get good marks in maths' and 'I don't like the way I look', does that imply causation? Why? Why not?

4. Open the dataset. Is there a relationship between age in months and grade point average? How strong is the relationship?

5. If there is a relationship between age in months and grade point average, does that imply causation? Why? Why not?

6. Above, I said that the correlation coefficient treats all relationships as linear, but not all are. Can you think of some examples of non-linear relationships that might occur in educational research?

▨ ▨ ▨ Further reading

Most good quantitative methods books contain sections on the correlation coefficient. Wonnacott, T.J. and Wonacott, R.J. (1990) *Introductory Statistics* (Wiley), gives a good overview.

An excellent book focusing solely on correlations is Chen, P. Y and Popovich, P. M. (2000) *Correlation: Parametric and Nonparametric Measures*, Quantitive Applications in the Social Sciences Series (Sage Publications).

■ ■ ■ Chapter 9

Multivariate analysis: using multiple linear regression to look at the relationship between several predictors and one dependent variable

■ ■ ■ Introduction

In the previous chapters we have looked at bivariate analysis, the relationship between two variables. In this chapter we will start to look at multivariate analyses, the relationship between more than two variables.

Why might we want to do that? In previous chapters we have looked at designing research questions and hypotheses. In many cases these can theoretically involve more than two variables. Say we wanted to look at factors that are related to low self-esteem among pupils. We would normally hypothesise that there are more than two such factors. For example, self-esteem may be affected by performance at school, popularity among peers, perceptions of physical attractiveness, parental socio-economic status (SES), gender and so on. Similarly, if we wanted to look at factors that affected whether or not boys performed well in school, we would hypothesise that there may be a number of variables that could affect this, such as ability, learning styles, school curriculum, SES and so on. We can obviously calculate separate correlations, t-tests or other bivariate measures between self-esteem and each of these measures. There is a big problem with doing this, however. If we look at the variables we say might predict boys' performance, we can see that many of them are likely to be related to one another.

For example, as I mentioned in Chapter 2, it is well known in educational research that there is a positive correlation between measures of parental SES and measures of ethnicity in that in many societies certain ethnic minority groups occupy the lower strata of the social class system. This gives us a problem when we look at bivariate correlations for these variables. If we looked at the relationship between achievement and ethnic group, we might well find that relationship to be significant. But, because there is also a relationship between socio-economic status and achievement, it is hard for us to know whether the relationship we found with ethnic group was due to the fact the pupils belong to different ethnic groups or to the fact that different ethnic groups are (on average) differentially positioned within the social class system. Therefore establishing cause and effect becomes particularly difficult. We said in Chapter 2 that we can only say with any confidence that A causes B when A comes before B in time, A is related to B and there is no third factor that is the cause of the relationship between A and B. This is something we can't determine using bivariate analyses. However, if we were able to put all the different variables we have measured into one analysis (e.g. both ethnicity and SES as predictors of achievement), and make sure that any measurement of the effect of, say, ethnicity on achievement takes account of the fact that both ethnicity and achievement are related to SES, then we would have a means of seeing whether ethnicity affects achievement when the fact that ethnic minority groups may have lower SES positions in society is taken into account. If we did that, any effect we found of ethnicity on achievement would be an effect that had taken into account the fact that part of the relationship was caused by the lower average SES of certain ethnic groups.

Multiple linear regression, which we will discuss in this chapter, will allow us to do this.

▧ ▧ ▧ What is multiple linear regression?

In multiple linear regression, we look at the relationship between one 'effect' variable, called the *dependent* or *outcome* variable, and one or more *predictors*, also called *independent* variables. A dependent variable could be, in our dataset for example, English grades. Theoretically, we would suggest a number of predictors: gender (girls tend to do better at reading than boys according to both research and state test data), parental SES (pupils from higher SES backgrounds usually score higher, thanks in part to better access to reading materials in the home) and self-concept in English (one would expect that there is a relationship between how good pupils think they are at English and their achievement in that subject, although the causality is unclear). Using regression analysis we will be able to test the hypothesis that these variables are predictors of English grades.

How regression works can best be demonstrated by looking at just two variables, for example English grades and maths grades. If we look at these variables, we can make a scatter plot that shows each child's maths grade on the x-axis, and each child's English grades on the y-axis (see Figure 9.1).

Regression works by trying to fit a straight line between these data points, so that the overall distance between the points and the line is minimised (it does this using a statistical method called least squares), in

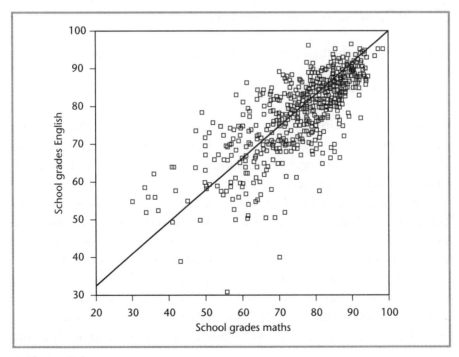

■ **Figure 9.1**
Scatter plot of English and maths scores.

this example the black line in Figure 9.1.

The basic regression equation is the following:

$$Y = a + bX$$

where:

- Y = the dependent variable;
- X = the predictor variable;
- a = the intercept, or the value of Y when X is zero (what English grades would a pupil be predicted to get if they scored a 0 in maths?). When you use more than two predictor variables, this value doesn't have a substantive interpretation and we can ignore it;
- b = the slope, or the value that Y will change by if X changes by 1 unit. For example, if X was maths grades, Y was English grades and b was 0.5, this would mean that when a pupil's maths grades go up by one, we would predict that their English grades go up by 0.5 points. This value is known as the regression *coefficient*.

When we use more than one predictor, our regression equation becomes:

$$Y = a + b_1X_1 + b_2X_2 + b_3X_3 + \ldots + B_nX_n$$

where b_1 is the coefficient for variable X_1, b_2 for variable X_2, etc. The interpretation is the same as when we had only one predictor, although obviously we cannot graph the relationship because we are now working in multidimensional space.

As well as giving us a coefficient, we can calculate a *p-value* which, as in correlation analysis, tells us whether or not the relationship is statistically significant (in other words, how likely it is that this relationship would exist in our sample if there was no relationship in the population).

As well as finding out whether the specific variables we have put in our analysis individually are related to the dependent variable, we might also want to know how well all our variables taken together (our model) predict the outcome. This is also calculated in regression analysis as the amount of variance in the dependent variable explained by all the predictors together. This measure is called *R square*.

Remembering how important levels of measurement are (is our variable nominal, ordinal or continuous?) and that different levels of measurement call for different types of analysis, you will be asking what type of variables we can use in regression analysis. Multiple linear regression requires the dependent variable to be continuous (although ordinal variables have also been used). Different types of regression analysis exist for nominal dependent variables (e.g. loglinear regression), but these go beyond this book. The predictor variables can be either continuous, ordinal or nominal, although if they are nominal we have to transform them if they have more than two categories (see below). If our predictors are ordinal, we have to be careful with our interpretation (again, we will discuss this further below).

Let's now have a look at how we can calculate regression in SPSS.

■ ■ ■ Doing regression analysis in SPSS

Let's see if we can predict English grades. Perhaps age in months (older pupils getting higher grades), family SES and family education level would be good predictors (from theory we would expect older children, children from higher SES households and children whose parents have higher education levels to do better).

To calculate a regression, we have to go through the following steps:

1. As usual, we choose 'Analyze'.
2. In the pop-down menu that appears we go to 'Regression'.
3. A new pop-down menu appears. We choose 'linear' (see Figure 9.2).
4. A new screen appears. From the list of variables on the left, we will first choose our dependent variable, in this case 'school grades English', and then click on the button next to 'Dependent'. The variable name now appears in the 'Dependent' box.

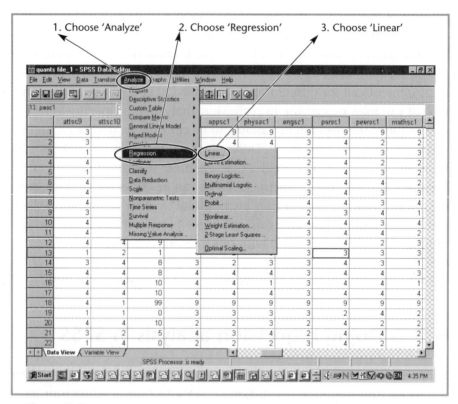

■ **Figure 9.2**
Multiple linear regression: steps 1–3.

5. Next, we have to choose our predictors. We choose 'family SES' and click on the arrow next to the 'Independent(s)' box. We do the same for family education and age in months. Then we click on 'OK' (see Figure 9.3).

The output screen now appears (see Figure 9.4). SPSS gives us a lot of output from a regression analysis. Not all of it is that relevant to us, though. Let's have a look at what it all means.

The first box of the output is labelled 'Variables Entered/Removed'. This is simply a list of all the predictors we have entered into the equation. It also gives the method we have used (more about that later).

The second box is labelled 'Model Summary'. This is an important one, as it gives us the measures of how well our overall model, i.e. our three predictors together, is able to predict English grades. The first measure in

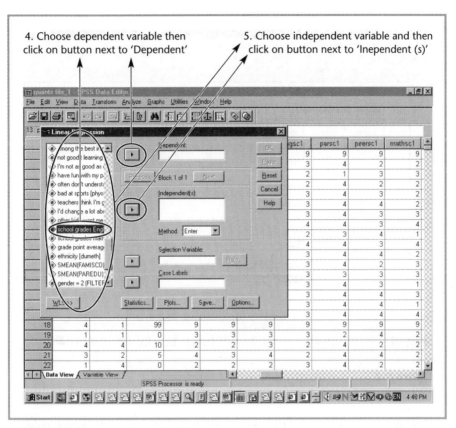

4. Choose dependent variable then click on button next to 'Dependent'

5. Choose independent variable and then click on button next to 'Inependent (s)'

■ **Figure 9.3**
Multiple regression: steps 4 and 5.

the table is called 'R'. This is a measure of how well our predictors predict the outcome, but we need to take the square root of R to get a more accurate measure. This is 'R square', which SPSS shows us in the next column. As I mentioned earlier on in this chapter, this gives us the amount of variance in English grades explained by the three predictor variables together. R square varies between 0 and 1. The next column is labelled 'Adjusted R Square'. This is, as the name implies, a correction to R square, which takes into account that we are looking at a sample rather than at the population. As the model is likely to fit the population less well than the sample, R square is adjusted downwards to give us a measure of how well our model is likely to fit in the population. Adjusted R square also lies between 0 and 1. In this case it is 0.110, which does not suggest that our predictors are particularly good at predicting English grades. Our model is

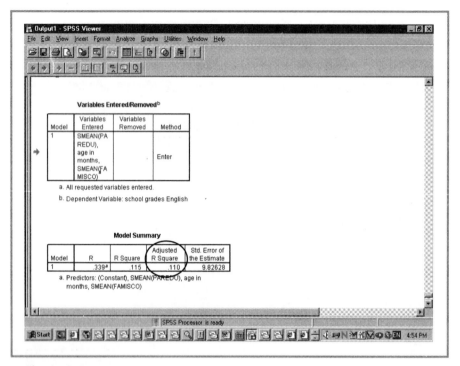

■ **Figure 9.4**
Regression output: part 1.

not a particularly good one. As a rough guide, the following rule of thumb can be used to see how well our model fits the data:

    <0.1: poor fit

    0.11–0.3: modest fit

    0.31–0.5: moderate fit

    > 0.5: strong fit

The final column gives us the standard error of the estimate. This is a measure of how much R is predicted to vary from one sample to the next.

The next output box is labelled ANOVA (see Figure 9.5). We will have a look at ANOVA in the next chapter, so we won't discuss it here.

The next box gives us some important information, and is where we will be able to look at the b, beta and significance of our three predictors separately.

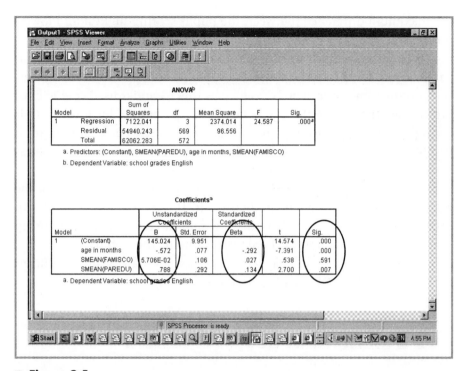

■ **Figure 9.5**
Regression output: part 2.

The first column gives us the names of our predictor variables. The variable labelled 'constant' is the intercept, or a (see above). The second column gives us our b coefficients, the value that Y will change by if X changes by 1 unit. If we look at age in months, that value is –0.572. So, in contrast to my hypothesis, if age in months goes up by one, English grades are predicted to go down by 0.572 (when, as here, the sign is negative, it means that if X increases, Y decreases). English grades are measured in percentages, so that's just over half a percentage point. In the next column, the standard error for each of these bs is given.

The following column contains the 'Beta' parameters. What is beta? One problem with b is that because variables are often measured using different scales, you can't use b values to see which of your variables has the strongest influence on the dependent variable. For example, parental SES might be measured on a ten-point scale, while age in months might be measured on a 24-point scale (due to grade retention). A b of 0.5 would then not be as strong an effect for parental SES as for age, because the maximum difference (between the pupils scoring highest and lowest on the scale) for SES would be 5 (10*0.5), while for age it would be 12 (24*0.5). That is why if we want to look at the *effect size* of each of our variables, we need to standardise the variables so that they are all measured on the same scale. The betas give us these standardised coefficients. We can see that while the b was largest for parental education, beta is strongest for age in months, at –0.292, followed by parental education (0.134) and parental SES (0.027). Betas vary between 0 and 1, with, as usual, 1 being the strongest effect.

The final column in this box gives us the statistical significance of the relationship between each predictor and the dependent variable. In other words, how likely it is that we would have found a relationship this strong in our sample if there wasn't one in the population. As you can see, age in months and parental education are statistically significant at the 0.01 level (<0.01), while parental SES is not.

▰ ▰ ▰ Methods of doing regression

When we looked at step 4 in doing our regression analysis in SPSS (see above), you might have noticed that underneath the box with the independent variables, there is an item labelled 'Method'. As you can see, the default method is called 'Enter'. What this basically means is that all the variables you have chosen as predictors are entered into the regression equation, and contribute to R square.

If you click on the arrow, you will see that there are three other options: 'Stepwise', Remove' and 'Backwards'. Basically, what all three do is, rather than include all the variables you have entered into the final model on which R square etc. are calculated, they only include the variables that are statistically significant.

This may seem like a good idea, especially if you have a lot of variables (that is why these procedures, and the stepwise procedure in particular, are quite popular), but there are serious problems with doing this.

Firstly, as you know, statistical significance is partly determined by sample size. Therefore, your sample size will partly determine which variables will be included and which not.

The second problem is slightly more complicated to explain, but is pretty serious. The program either adds (in 'Stepwise') the variable that is most significant in the first step, then the second most significant in the second step, and so on (or removes the least significant in step one and so on, in 'Remove'). This may sound unproblematic, but remember that most of your predictors will be related to one another at least to a certain extent (think of parental education and SES in our example). This causes a number of problems:

■ the regression coefficients for the selected variables will be too large (because of the removal of the other variables);

■ R square will be biased (upwards);

■ the p-values will be biased;

■ and finally, and possibly most importantly, you are replacing theory and judgement as a researcher by a mechanical process.

As you can see, these problems are serious, so my advice would be too stick to the 'Enter' default.

■ ■ ■ Using ordinal and nominal variables as predictors

In theory, regression analysis is designed to be used with continuous variables. Both the dependent and the independent variables are supposed to be continuous. This obviously limits the extent to which this method can be used to construct models that properly explain the variance in the dependent variable. In our example, this means that there are a number of variables we can't use, like all the variables on pupil attitude (which are ordinal) and the variables that are nominal, like gender.

Ordinal predictors

Luckily, regression as a method is what we call 'robust'. This means that it works quite well when certain assumptions have not been met. In

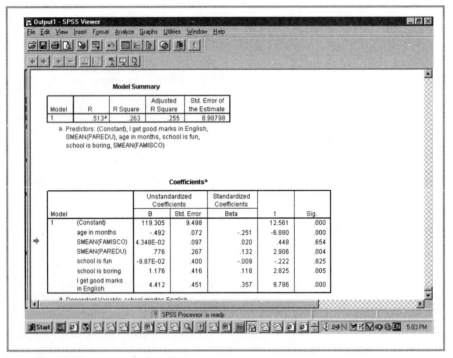

▨ Figure 9.6
Output including two ordinal variables.

practice, we can even use ordinal variables in our regression analyses quite successfully. This is good news, as there are a number of ordinal variables which might well be good predictors of English language grades, for example how good pupils think they are at English and what they think about school.

Let's add a couple of these. We will go back into 'Analyze', choose 'Regression', then 'Linear' and add 'I get good marks in English', 'school is fun' and 'school is boring' to the independent variables list along with age in months and parental education and SES. This gives us the output shown in Figure 9.6.

When we look at the model summary, we can see that this has made a difference: our adjusted r squared is up to 0.255, a modest relationship. When we look at the 'Coefficients' box, we can see that it is the variables 'I get good marks in English' and 'I often don't understand things in English' that have made a difference. Both are statistically significant, and 'I get good marks in English' has the largest beta of all variables in the analysis (0.357). If pupils' score on that variable goes up by 1 (from 'Agree' to 'Agree totally', for example), English grades are predicted to go up by 4.4. Here I must add a note of warning. As you know, one of the problems with ordinal variables compared to continuous variables is that the distance between the scale points is not exactly fixed. Therefore, we need to be very cautious in interpreting b. As the distance between, for example, point 1 ('Disagree totally') and point 2 ('Disagree') on the scale is not necessarily the same as that between point 2 ('Disagree') and point 3 ('Agree'), we have to question what exactly our b coefficient means. An important thing you may have noticed is that now we have added these new variables, the coefficients for our three original predictors have changed a bit. This reminds us that any model we test is only as good as the variables we include, and the coefficients we find will change if other variables are added.

Nominal predictors

The situation with regard to nominal variables is a bit more complicated. Because they are not ordered, we have to create something called *dummy variables* before we can use them in regression. What does this mean? Basically, what we are going to have to do is compare the categories to one another. For example, if we look at our variable school type, we need to compare Catholic, local authority and local authority (COE) schools. To achieve this, what we need to do is make one category into our reference category to which the others are going to be compared. Let's take state schools as our reference category in this example. We are first going to compare children in Catholic schools with children in state schools, and then children in local authority schools with children in state schools. How do we do this? We will have to make two new variables, one for Catholic and one for local authority schools. We will have to recode our variable school type so that all Catholic schools are coded as 1, and all other schools as 0. Then we need to make another new variable, where all our local authority schools are coded 1 and all other schools are coded 0. How do we do that in SPSS?

1. On the top bar, choose 'Transform'.
2. In the pop-down menu that appears, choose 'Recode'.

3. A new menu appears that gives us two choices: 'Into Same Variables' and 'Into Different Variables'. If we choose 'Into Same Variables', our original variable will be changed (and we won't be able to change it back). If we choose 'Into Different Variables' a new variable will be created, and our original variable will stay the same. This is what we want to do, so we choose 'Into Different Variables' (see Figure 9.7).

4. A new screen appears. This is our recode screen. The first thing we have to do is select the variable we want to recode, in this case school type, and then click on the arrow. The variable appears in the first box.

5. The next thing we need to do is give the new variable a new name. We type the new name under 'Name' (lets call this variable 'catholic') and press change. In the box, the arrow now points to 'catholic' instead of to a question mark.

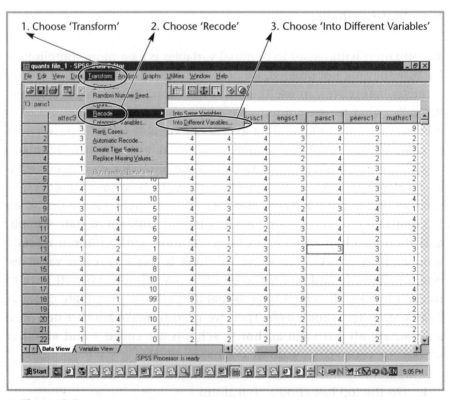

▧ **Figure 9.7**
Transforming variables: steps 1–3.

6. Now we can give the new variable a label, for example 'catholic or not'. We need to add this to the 'Label' box. Next, we choose 'Continue'.

7. Now we have to tell SPSS what the new and old values are. To do this, we press the 'Old and New Values' button (see Figure 9.8).

8. A new box appears. In this box we have to specify the old and new values (recodes) for our new variable. The first thing we need to do is put our first 'old' value into the 'Value' box. Catholic schools were coded '2', so we fill in 2.

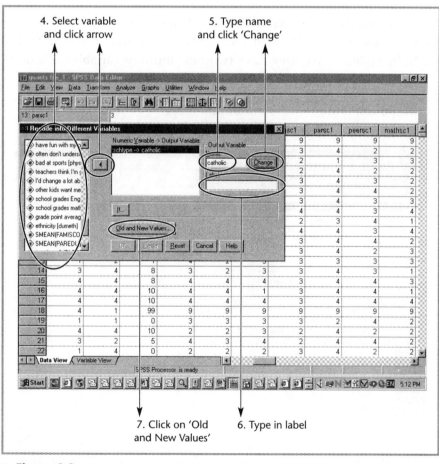

■ **Figure 9.8**
Recoding variables: steps 4–7.

9. Next, we need to fill in the new value for that code. We said that Catholic would be coded 1, so that is what we fill in as value in the 'New Value' box.

10. We press 'Add'. In the 'Old – New' boxes we can now see that we are turning code 2 into code 1.

11. Next, we have to give our state schools, coded 1, and our local authority schools, coded 3, the new code 0. We do this in the same way.

12. We press 'Continue' (see Figure 9.9).

13. And finally, 'OK'. If we look at the 'Variable View', we will see that a new variable has been added to the end of the list.

We now need to do the same to make a new dummy variable for our local authority schools, with local authority coded 1 and state and Catholic coded 0. We now have two new dummy variables. We don't

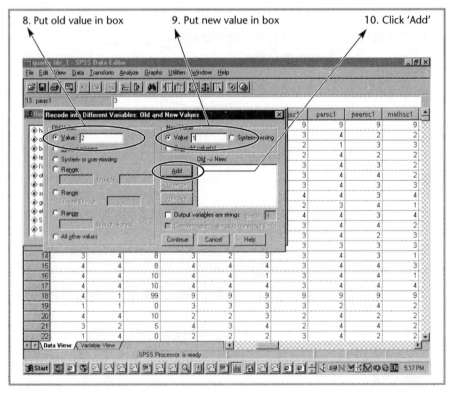

▨ **Figure 9.9**
Recoding variables: steps 8–10.

make a dummy variable for state because that is our reference variable, the one we are comparing the other two to. This means that when we are using nominal variables in regression, we will always have to make as many dummy variables as there are categories in the nominal variable minus one (the reference variable). When we have a nominal variable with just two categories (like gender), all we need to do is code one category 1, and the other 0 (for ease of interpretation), and then we can use the variable in our regression analysis.

Let's add these two dummy variables ('catholic' and 'local authority') to our regression, and see what results we get. As is shown in Figure 9.10, adding these variables has not increased explained variance. When we look at the coefficients, we can see that the b for Catholic is 0.316 and that for local authority (COE) –0.713. This means that pupils in Catholic schools are predicted to do slightly better than those in state schools, while pupils in local authority schools are predicted to do slightly worse. The beta's are small, though (0.012 and –0.032 respectively), and neither variable is significant, so school type does not seem to be a significant factor.

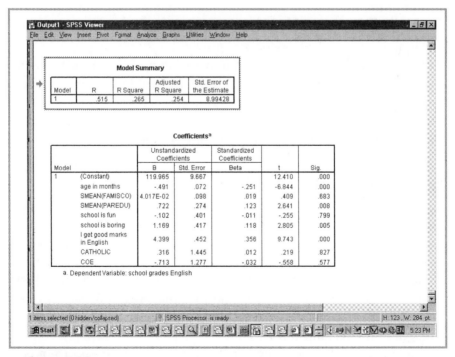

Model Summary

Model	R	R Square	Adjusted R Square	Std. Error of the Estimate
1	.515	.265	.254	8.99428

Coefficients[a]

Model		Unstandardized Coefficients		Standardized Coefficients		
		B	Std. Error	Beta	t	Sig.
1	(Constant)	119.965	9.667		12.410	.000
	age in months	-.491	.072	-.251	-6.844	.000
	SMEAN(FAMISCO)	4.017E-02	.098	.019	.409	.683
	SMEAN(PAREDU)	.722	.274	.123	2.641	.008
	school is fun	-.102	.401	-.011	-.255	.799
	school is boring	1.169	.417	.118	2.805	.005
	I get good marks in English	4.399	.452	.356	9.743	.000
	CATHOLIC	.316	1.445	.012	.219	.827
	COE	-.713	1.277	-.032	-.558	.577

a. Dependent Variable: school grades English

■ **Figure 9.10**
Output including dummy variables.

▪ ▪ ▪ The dependent variable

We have now seen that multiple regression is a very flexible method when it comes to what independent variables we can use. With some tweaking we can use continuous, ordinal or nominal (dummy) variables.

What about the dependent variable? There the situation is a bit different. In traditional multiple linear regression the dependent variable has to be continuous.

What do we do when we have ordinal or nominal dependent variables? Luckily, special methods of regression have been developed for use with that type of dependent variable. When you go into 'Analyze', and then choose 'Regression', you will see that the pop-down menu contains methods such as binary logistic regression, multinominal logistic regression, ordinal and probit. The first two are for use with nominal dependent variables, the latter two with ordinal dependent variables.

▪ ▪ ▪ Diagnostics in regression

As with most other methods, a number of conditions need to be met before we can use regression analysis with confidence. The two most important conditions are that the relationship between independent and dependent variables must be linear and that the independent variables shouldn't be too strongly correlated to one another.

Linearity and outliers

This method is not called multiple linear regression for nothing. Multiple linear regression imposes a linear relationship on the data points that describe the relationship between the two variables (see Figure 9.1). If the relationship is non-linear, the model will not fit the data properly. There are many relationships that are not linear, for example where we need to pass a threshold to find any effect or where the strength of the relationship tails off.

One way of finding out whether the relationship is linear or not is by looking at how many large *residuals* there are. What is a residual?

Basically, a residual is the observed value of the dependent variable minus the value predicted by the regression equation, for each case. Or, in other words, how well does our model (which draws a straight line through the data) predict the value of the dependent variable for an individual case? If we look at Figure 9.1, we can see that regression draws a straight line through the data points. This is our predicted regression line. Each individual point (which represents the scores of an individual on the two variables) can be close or further away from that line. The closer to the line, the better the score of that person is predicted by the model. The further away, the worse our prediction. The higher our residual, the further away from the regression line the data point is. Obviously, we want to have as few high residuals as possible, because having many high residuals would suggest that our model does not fit the data, possibly because our relationship is not linear. We can easily check this in SPSS.

When going through the steps to do a regression analysis (see above), we need to do something additional following step 5:

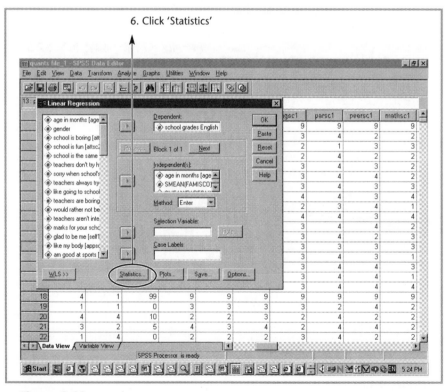

■ **Figure 9.11**
Diagnostics: part 1.

6. At the bottom of the box is a button labelled 'Statistics' (see Figure 9.11). We click on it.

7. A new window appears (see Figure 9.12). At the bottom of that window is a box labelled 'Residuals'. In that box, we need to tick the box next to 'Casewise diagnostics'. When we do this, a new box saying 'Outliers outside 3 standard deviations' is highlighted. We want to stick to this default, so just press 'Continue' and 'OK'.

When we look at the output (see Figure 9.13), we can see that a new box has appeared at the end of the output, labelled 'Casewise Diagnostics'. This lists all the cases with a standardised residual more than 3 standard deviations away from the predicted score. These are cases for which the predictors predict the value of the dependent variable (scores in English) very badly. In this case, there is one, with a residual of –4.075. This means that this one

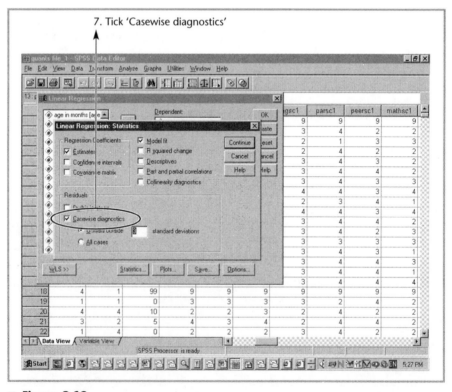

▨ **Figure 9.12**
Diagnostics: part 2.

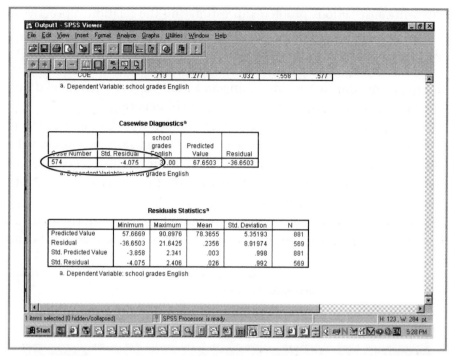

■ **Figure 9.13**
Outliers casewise diagnostics output.

pupil has done very much worse in English than we would have predicted on the basis of our model (i.e. age, parental education, parental SES, school is fun, school is boring, I get good marks in English and school type). One outlier, as such cases are known, is clearly unproblematic in a sample of over 800 – humans being unpredictable, there will always be some outliers. We need to worry when the number of outliers rises to, say, 10 per cent of the sample. In such a case our model is not fitting the data well. Non-linearity may be one reason for this. The final box in the output, called 'Residuals Statistics', gives us some summary data on the residuals (unstandardised and standardised). We don't need to worry about that too much, as this does not provide us with any essential information.

Multicollinearity

A second major precondition is that our predictor (or independent) variables mustn't be too strongly correlated with one another. If they are, this will cause serious problems in estimating the relationship between the dependent and predictor variables because it becomes hard to calculate the individual contribution of each variable. When predictor variables are very highly correlated, we have to wonder whether they are not in fact measuring the same thing and would be better combined into one new variable. This problem is called *multicollinearity*.

How can we find out if we have multicollinearity? We can get SPSS to give us some diagnostics on this as well. Once again we click on the 'Statistics' button (see step 6 above). Then, in the 'Statistics' box, we tick the box marked 'Collinearity diagnostics' on the left (see Figure 9.14). Click 'Continue', and then 'OK'.

Once we have done this, some more output appears (see Figure 9.15). If we look in the 'Coefficients' box, we can see that as well as b, beta and

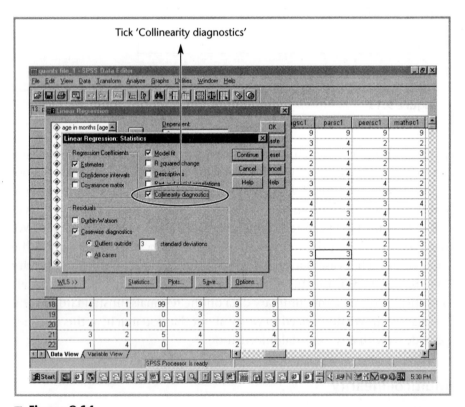

▨ **Figure 9.14**
Collinearity diagnostics

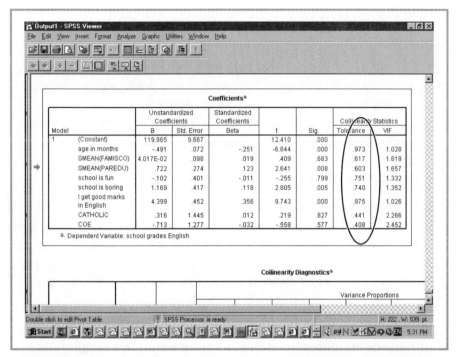

▦ Figure 9.15
Collinearity diagnostics output.

significance, we now have two boxes labelled 'Collinearity Statistics', one called 'Tolerance' and one called 'VIF'. These two measures do essentially exactly the same thing, so we will just discuss one, tolerance. Tolerance is the amount of variance in the individual variable *not* explained by the other predictor variables. It varies from 0 to 1. A value close to 1 indicates that the other predictors do not explain the variance in that variable. A value close to 0 suggests that almost all the variance in the variable (for example, parental education) is explained by the other variables (here age, parental SES, school is fun, school is boring, I get good marks in English and school type). In our example there are no serious problems as no tolerance values are close to 0. Most variables have a tolerance of >0.6; only local authority and catholic give us some cause for concern, with a tolerance of around 0.4. Dummy variables will often have low tolerances because they explain one another.

▪ ▪ ▪ Common misconceptions

1. *My regression model fits the data well. That means that my predictors cause my dependent variable, doesn't it?* No. Regression is basically a correlational method, and as I have mentioned previously, correlation does not mean causation. When we do regression analyses, we are easily tempted to think in causal terms, but the method does not determine that, it only looks at mathematical relationships. Any causal inference must come from our theorising.

2. *If my dependent variable is not continuous, I can use it in my regression analyses if I turn it into a dummy variable, can't I?* No, you can only use dummy variables for predictor (independent) variables. If your dependent variable is not continuous, you need to use other types of regression, for example logit and probit regression for nominal and ordinal dependent variables respectively.

3. *The variable with the highest b is the one that has the strongest relationship with the dependent variable, isn't it?* B tells us by how much Y (the dependent variable) will change if X (the independent variable) goes up by one unit. Because different independent variables are often measured using different scales (e.g. a four-point scale and a ten point scale), you can't say on the basis of b which variable is most strongly related to Y. To do this you need to standardise them (that will give you beta).

4. *The variable with the lowest significance level is the one that has the strongest relationship with the dependent variable, isn't it?* The significance level merely tells us how likely it is for us to find a relationship of that size in our sample if there is no relationship in the population. Again, we need to look at beta to see which independent variable is related most strongly to the dependent variable.

5. *If X goes up by 1, Y goes up by the value of beta, doesn't it?* No, that is only the case for b. Beta, the standardised version of b, allows us to compare the effect size of the different independent variables. This is because standardisation means that they are all measured using the same scale.

6. *If my model predicts my dependent variable well, then my coefficients (b, beta) accurately reflect the relationship between my predictor and dependent variables.* Not necessarily. Regression can only measure what we put in. If we added other (not now included) variables to our model, the coefficients for the variables that were already in the model may well change.

7. *If I have a tolerance of 0, that means that I don't have multicollinearity, doesn't it?* No, it's the other way round. Tolerance is the amount of variance in the individual variable *not* explained by the other predictor variables. A value close to 1 indicates that the other predictors do not explain the variance in that variable. A value close to 0 suggests that almost all the variance in the variable is explained by the other variables.

■ ■ ■ Summary

In this chapter we have started to do some multivariate analyses. We looked at the relationship between one dependent and several independent variables.

In multiple linear regression, we look at the relationship between one 'effect' variable, called the *dependent* or *outcome* variable, and one or more *predictors*, also called *independent* variables.

Regression analysis allows us to do a number of things. Firstly, we can look at how well all our predictor variables together predict the outcome variable. R square will give us a statistic (between 0 and 1) that will tell us that. Secondly, we can look at the relationship between each of our predictors separately and the outcome variable. For each predictor we can calculate a relationship that takes into account the effect of all the other independent variables. B gives us the amount the dependent variable changes by if our predictor goes up by 1. Beta is a standardised version that allows us to compare which of our predictors has the strongest relationship with the outcome variable. The significance of the relationship is also calculated.

In multiple linear regression, the independent variables can be continuous, ordinal or nominal (if we use dummy variables). The dependent variable must be continuous.

■ ■ ■ Exercises

1. You want to find out what factors predict achievement in mathematics. Develop a model that you think can explain this.
2. Calculate your model in SPSS. What is R square, and what does it mean?
3. Calculate your model in SPSS. What is your b and what does it mean?
4. Calculate your model in SPSS. What is beta, and what does it mean?
5. Calculate your model in SPSS. What is the p-value, and what does it mean?
6. If you find a model that fits well, does that mean your predictors cause your dependent variable? Why? Why not?
7. What is a dummy variable, and when do you use it?
8. When would you use regression rather than correlation?

■ ■ ■ Further reading

Regression analysis is covered in most statistics textbooks, but there are also quite a few texts that deal specifically with the topic.

Pedhazur, E. J. (2000) *Multiple Regression in Behavioral Research* (Wadsworth Publishing) gives an excellent, if quite technical overview of regression techniques.

Cohen, P. (ed.) (2002) *Applied Multiple Regression: Correlation for the Social Sciences* (Lawrence Erlbaum) is a comprehensive overview of regression and correlation.

■ ■ ■ Chapter 10

Using analysis of variance to compare more than two groups

In Chapter 7 we looked at how we can compare two groups, for example an experimental and a control group, using the t-test. In many cases we might want to compare more than two groups. Imagine that we have designed an intervention to improve the teaching of science that takes two forms: in the first form (type A) teachers are sent on a six-day course; in the second form (type B) teachers are sent on a three-day course followed by peer coaching. We might want to find out which intervention is the most effective in terms of improving pupil test scores in science. We could divide participants into two groups that take each type of intervention and compare them to teachers in a matched comparison group. This would give us three groups. We can then test pupils in the classes of teachers in the three groups before and after the intervention, and calculate a gain score (after – before for each child). What we will then want to do is compare all three groups, because we will want to know both whether the intervention as a whole has been effective, and whether or not type A of the intervention (six-day course) has been more effective than type B (three-day course and peer coaching).

To do this we can use a method called *analysis of variance*, often called by its abbreviation *ANOVA*.

■ ■ ■ What is ANOVA?

Analysis of variance is a method that allows us to compare the mean score of a continuous (or ordinal with many scale points) variable between a number of groups, for example the two interventions and control group mentioned above. What ANOVA does is test the null hypothesis that several group means (the mean score of pupils in type A intervention classrooms, type B intervention classrooms and comparison classrooms) are equal in the population. You may wonder why the method is called analysis of variance when we want to compare the means. This is because ANOVA works by comparing the spread (or variance) of the group means (called the *between-groups sum of squares*) with the spread (or variance) of values within the groups (called the *within-group sum of squares*). If the variance of the group means is larger than you would predict from looking at the within-group variance, then it is likely that the means differ. So, in our example, ANOVA will calculate the variance of achievement scores within type A, type B and comparison groups, calculate the variance of the three mean scores, and then see whether the variance of these three means is larger than we would predict from looking at the within group variances.

In ANOVA we can use one or more independent variables, but they all have to be nominal or ordinal. If the independent variables have more than five groups, ANOVA quickly starts to loose its power to discriminate between them.

ANOVA, like regression, is quite a flexible method and can do a number of different tasks. The first thing we will want to know, when comparing our two treatments and our comparison group, is whether there are any overall differences between the three groups. To do this, ANOVA compares the mean scores on the dependent variable (in this example changes in science test scores) between the three groups (type A intervention, type B intervention, no intervention). In a similar way to what was done when we compared two groups using the t-test, ANOVA uses a test (the F-test) to determine whether there are significant differences between the means of the three groups. Once the F-test statistics are calculated, we can calculate a p-value, which, as usual, tells us how likely it is for us to find differences between the means of our three groups that are this large in our sample if there were no difference between the three groups in the population. As usual, a cut off point of <0.05 is used as a rule of thumb to determine whether or not our relationship is significant (although with larger samples, <0.01 and <0.001 are also sometimes used, which points once again to the essential arbitrariness of these cut-off points).

One important thing to note about the F-test is that it is a global test. What that means is that if we find a significant difference (p-value <0.05) all we know is that overall there is a significant difference somewhere in the comparisons between the three groups. We don't know where the significance lies. It could be that the means of all three groups differ significantly from one another, or it could be that both intervention groups (type A and type B) differ from the comparison group, or that only one does, and so on. Clearly, that is a bit frustrating, and we will want to find a way of telling us which comparisons (type A with type B, type A with comparison, type B with comparison, etc.) are significantly different.

Luckily a number of tests have been developed that allow us to do just that. These tests are called *post hoc comparisons*. As we will see when we start looking at how to do ANOVA in SPSS, there are at least a dozen such tests in existence, which all do individual comparisons between the groups of our independent variable. We are not going to discuss all these tests here but just look at one of the most commonly used ones.

The Scheffe test compares the mean score on the outcome variable for each group with that for each other group. So, for example, the mean achievement score for pupils taught by type A intervention teachers will be compared to the mean score of those taught by type B intervention teachers and to the mean score of no intervention teachers. The type B mean score will also be compared to the non-intervention mean. A significance level (p-value) is calculated for each test. This will allow us to see which contrasts are actually significantly different and which aren't. Once we have done some examples in SPSS this will become clearer.

So far, we have only discussed doing ANOVA when we have just one predictor. As I mentioned above, you can also test a model with several predictors. In such situations, what ANOVA will do is calculate a separate test for each predictor variable and do separate post hoc comparisons for each as well. An overall R square assessing how well the model as a whole (all predictors) predict the outcome is also provided.

■ ■ ■ Doing ANOVA in SPSS

ANOVA is quite a complicated method, so it's a good idea to start having a look at how we can do an ANOVA in practice using SPSS, as this should clarify some of the difficulties. We are going to have a look at the relationship between pupil achievement (grade point average) and school environment quality (coded as high, medium or low and measured by the researcher looking at a number of factors connected to school environment such as tidiness and repair of buildings). Our hypothesis would be that students in schools with a more highly rated quality of environment will have a higher grade point average. What do we need to do?

1. As usual, we have to start by going into 'Analyze'.

2. Next we go into 'General Linear Model'.

3. A new pop-down menu appears. We choose 'Univariate' (see Figure 10.1).

4. A new box appears called 'Univariate'. This is where we are going to specify our dependent and independent variables. The first thing we need to do is choose our dependent variable. In the list of variables we select 'grade point average' and click on the arrow next to 'Dependent'. Grade point average now appears in the 'Dependent' box.

5. Next, we need to choose our independent variable. In ANOVA this is called the 'Fixed Factor'. From the list of variables we choose 'quality of school environment' and click on the arrow next to 'Fixed Factor(s)'. The variable now appears in that box.

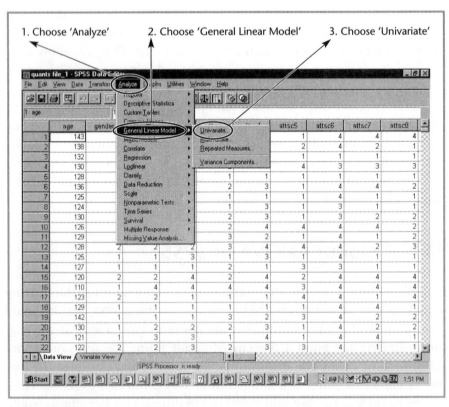

■ **Figure 10.1**
ANOVA: steps 1–3.

6. We would also like to look at some contrasts between the three groups, using the Scheffe test. To do that, we need to click the button on the left labelled 'Post Hoc' (see Figure 10.2).

7. Once we have done that, a new box appears. The first thing we need to do is to select the independent variables for which we want to compare the categories. As we only have one independent variable in our analyses, we just need to select it (by clicking on the name), and click the arrow next to it. The variable now appears in the box labelled 'Post Hoc Tests for'.

8. Next we need to specify which test we want to use. Many possible tests are listed but we will stick to Scheffe and tick that box (see Figure 10.3). We then press 'Continue' and 'OK'.

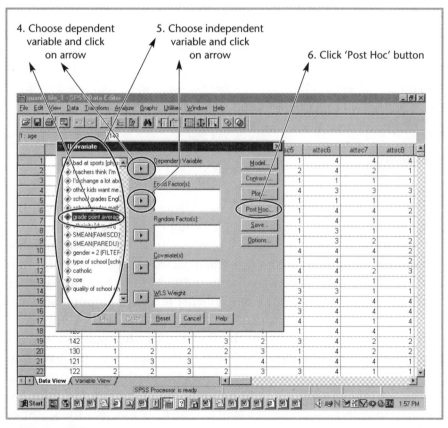

■ **Figure 10.2**
ANOVA: steps 4–6.

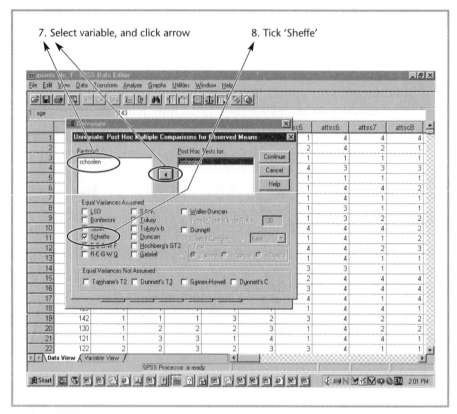

7. Select variable, and click arrow   8. Tick 'Sheffe'

■ **Figure 10.3**
ANOVA: steps 7 and 8.

Now lets have a look at the output (see Figure 10.4). As is so often the case, SPSS will give us a lot of output, not all of which we actually need.

The first box, labelled 'Between-Subjects Factors', just lists the number of respondents in the three groups. The important information is given in the next box 'Tests of Between-Subjects Effects'. This is going to tell us whether our variable (school environment) is related to pupil achievement. This is quite a complicated bit of output so we will go through it bit by bit. The first row gives us the statistics for the total model. This contains all our independent variables. In this case, we only have one (school environment). The next row lists the statistics for something called 'Intercept'. This is our within-group sum of squares, the value we are comparing our model to (see above). The next row lists the statistics for the independent variable (school environment). If we had other independent variables in our model those would be listed here too. The columns list the different statistics in ANOVA. The first gives the sum of

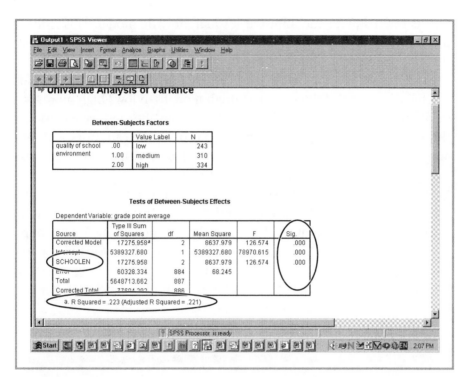

■ **Figure 10.4**
ANOVA output: part 1.

squares (within and between groups), the second from last the F-test value. The one we are really interested in is the last one, the significance level or p-value. Once again, if the p-value is below 0.05, we conventionally say our value is significant (unlikely to occur in the sample if there is no effect in the population). When we look at this column, we can see that the within-group sum of squares or intercept (the individual variance within the groups) is highly significant. This basically means that pupils have different grade point averages and is something we already knew. The interesting information is contained in the other two values. Firstly, we can see that our variable, school environment, is significant. This means that there is a significant difference between the groups, though we don't know between which groups (high more than low? high more than medium? medium more than low? all?). The values for the total (called 'Corrected Model') in this case are the same as for our variable, because our model only contains that variable. Once we have more than one predictor, that will no longer be the case (see below). One interesting additional piece of information is given just below the table.

This is the R square and adjusted R square for the model. This is interpreted in the same way as in regression and our value of 0.22 suggests that our one variable model modestly predicts achievement.

Next, we can have a look at the post hoc tests (see Figure 10.5), which will tell us where the differences lie (high more than low? high more than medium? medium more than low? all?). The post hoc test we are using is the Scheffe test. These give us comparisons of all the categories with one another. Let's have a look at the box labelled 'Multiple Comparisons'. Once again there is a lot of output but we won't need to look at all of it. In the first column we can see that the mean for the low group is compared to the mean of the medium and of the high groups. The mean of the medium group is compared to the means of the low and high groups, and the mean for the high group is compared to the means of the low and medium groups. Of the other columns, we are only going to look at the second, labelled 'Mean Difference' and the fourth, labelled 'Sig.'.

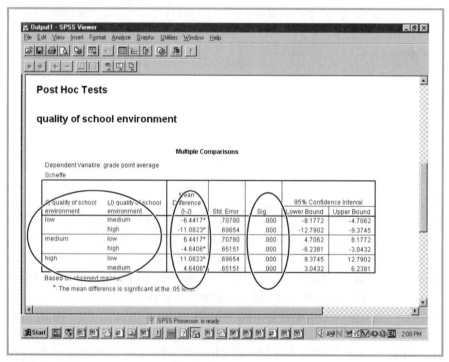

▇ **Figure 10.5**
ANOVA output: part 2 – multiple comparisons.

The mean difference does exactly what it says on the tin: it gives us the difference between the means of the different categories. So, for example, we can see that the difference in mean between low and medium is –6.4417. This means that the mean grade point average (GPA) of children in schools with a low-rated school environment is more than six points lower than the mean GPA of children in medium-rated schools. It is also 11 points lower than the mean of children in high-rated schools.

The column labelled 'Sig.' gives us our p-values. If we look at this column, we can see that all our p-values are highly significant, so it is likely that all three groups differ from one another. Pupils in a high-rated school environment have the highest mean GPA, followed by those in medium-rated schools and those in low-rated schools. Of course, this doesn't take into account the fact that these differences may be caused by other variables not included in the analyses (maybe the high-rated schools are in more middle-class areas, for example).

What the Scheffe test also does is put the variables into groups which have a similar mean score on the dependent variable. These are called 'Homogeneous Subsets' (see Figure 10.6). In this case, because all three

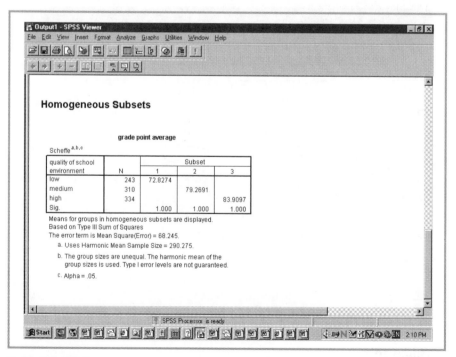

■ **Figure 10.6**
ANOVA output: part 3 – homogeneous subgroups.

groups differ significantly, there are three such subsets or groups. Group one contains the 'low' category. The mean GPA for pupils in that group is 72.8. Group 2 contains the medium-rated schools. The mean score for children in that group is 79.3. The final group is the high-rated schools. The mean score for that group is 83.9.

■ ■ ■ The effect size measure

As I have mentioned before, we need to look at the effect size as well as statistical significance so we can compare the strength of the effect of different variables (and across different studies). Our effect size index in ANOVA is called *eta squared*, and is calculated by dividing the within-groups sum of squares by the total sum of squares. Eta squared varies between 0 and 1 and

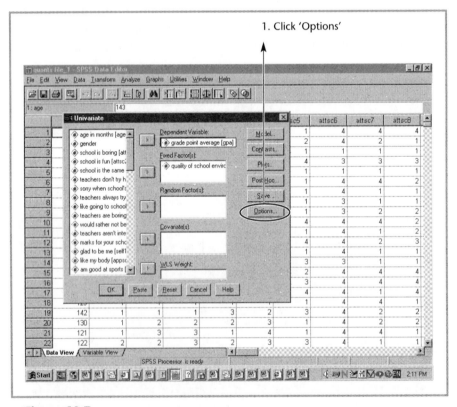

■ **Figure 10.7**

ANOVA: producing effect size measures – part 1.

is interpreted in the usual way, i.e. 0–0.1 is a weak effect, 0.1–0.3 is a modest effect, 0.3–0.5 is a moderate effect and >0.5 is a strong effect (remember though that these cut-off points are just guidelines).

In SPSS, eta squared can be calculated as follows. Following step 5 above, in the 'Univariate' box, we click on the button labelled 'Options' on the left of the screen (see Figure 10.7). A new box appears (see Figure 10.8). Under 'display', we tick 'Estimates of effect size'.

When we then press 'Continue' and 'OK', the output appears (see Figure 10.9). One thing has changed: in the second box, labelled 'Tests of Between-Subjects Effects', a new column has appeared, called 'Partial Eta Squared'. This is our effect size index. If we look at the values, we can see that the value for our variable, school environment, is 0.22, a modest effect size. The value for the within-groups sum of squares (intercept) is 0.99, which means that there is a lot of variance in children's grade point averages.

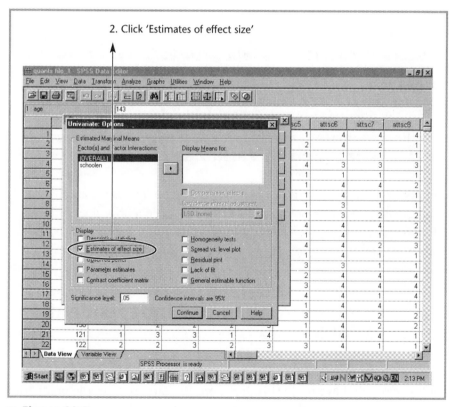

■ **Figure 10.8**
ANOVA: producing effect size measures – part 2.

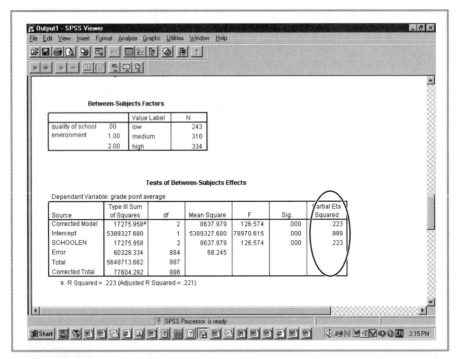

■ **Figure 10.9**
Effect size output.

■ ■ ■ What kind of variables can we use?

In ANOVA, our dependent variable has to be continuous or ordinal with many categories. Our predictors have to be nominal or ordinal with not too many categories. If we had too many categories, the number of contrasts would become too large and lead to results hard to interpret.

■ ■ ■ Using more than one independent variable

So far we have only used one independent variable in our analyses. We don't necessarily have to do this, however. We can use multiple predictors in ANOVA models, just like we did in regression. What will then happen is that, as in regression, we can look at both the fit of the total model and at the significance and effect sizes of the individual variables. Another useful thing that we can do in ANOVA is look at so-called 'interaction effects'. What is an interaction effect? When we have a significant interaction effect it means that the effect of one variable on another, for example assessment method on pupil outcomes, is different for different conditions of a third variable. For example, if we were looking at the effect of assessment methods, it may be that boys do better using exams while girls do better when essay-style assessment is used. In order to capture this kind of effect in ANOVA, we can introduce interaction effects which allow us to see whether the relationship between independent and dependent variables is mediated in any way by third variables. All additional variables have to be nominal or ordinal with a limited number of categories.

What do we need to do in ANOVA to get more than one independent variable and interaction effects? It is quite simple. All we need to do is add more than one variable to the independent variables list after step 5 above. ANOVA will automatically calculate any interaction effects. All the other steps are exactly the same as before. We will see what happens when we include school type as well as school environment as a predictor.

Let's have a look at the output (see Figure 10.10). When we look at the 'Test of Between-Subjects Effects' box, we can see first of all that our model

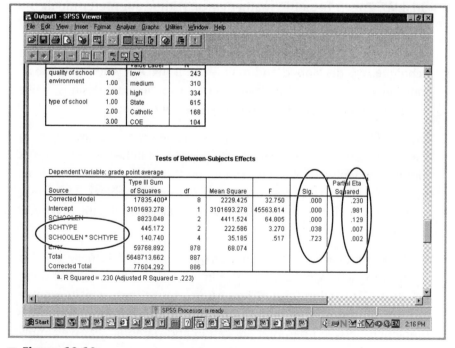

■ **Figure 10.10**
Multiple predictors and interaction effects: output.

as a whole (the row labelled 'Corrected Model') is statistically significant, with an adjusted R squared of 0.23 (this is given just below the box).

If we look at our two predictor variables, we can see that school environment and school type are both significantly related to achievement (in the 'Sig.' column) at the 0.05 level. The effect of school environment is modest (partial eta squared is 0.13 – see last column), while the effect of school type may be statistically significant, but it is very weak (an eta of only 0.007). The interaction effect is not significant. This means that we can't say that quality of school environment has more of an effect in one type of school (e.g. state schools) than it does in another (e.g. Catholic schools).

■ ■ ■ ANOVA and regression

You may have noticed that ANOVA and regression appear to do many of the same things (both look at the relationship between several independent or predictor variables and a continuous outcome or dependent variable). This is because, mathematically, they are pretty much the same, both being part of what is known as the 'general linear model'.

What then are the differences? The main one lies in the field where the technique was developed and mainly used. ANOVA, with its comparisons between groups, was developed for experimental designs, while regression was developed for non-experimental research.

Regression is more flexible than ANOVA, however. As we have seen, in ANOVA we can only use variables with a limited number of categories as our independent variables. Regression, on the contrary, can include all types of variables (through the use of dummy variables). Therefore, while regression is suitable for the analysis of all types of data, ANOVA is more limited.

What about interaction? Is that not unique to ANOVA? Actually, no. It is very easy to include interaction terms in regression. All we need to do to include an interaction term of two variables is to make a new variable that is the product of the two. If, for example, we wanted to look at the interaction between parental education and parental SES, we simply need to make a new variable by multiplying parental SES by parental education (new variable = parental SES * parental education) and add this variable to our regression model.

Regression also allows us to look at different types of outcome variables (using logit and probit regression, for example), and has several important extensions (such as multilevel modelling and structural equation modelling) that we will discuss later. It is also easier to compute.

If regression then can do everything ANOVA can and more, why use ANOVA? Why bother to discuss it in this book? The main reason is that, conceptually, ANOVA fits experimental designs well. Also, in some cases researchers, especially those schooled in experimental techniques, may be used to teaching and using ANOVA, and may therefore not yet have switched to regression methods. As for why we have included regression in this book, the reason is simply that as you will still see ANOVA used often, it is important that you know what it is and how to use it.

■ ■ ■ Common misconceptions

1. *Analysis of variance tests whether the variances in the different groups are equal, doesn't it?* Not quite. While the method is called analysis of variance because of the statistical calculations it uses, we are actually comparing whether or not the means of the dependent variables are equal in our different groups.

2. *The p-value is the test of statistical significance, and the F-test gives us our effect size, doesn't it?* Well, while the p-value does indeed give us the statistical significance, the effect size index is eta squared. The F-test is a statistical test like the t-test, used to calculate our significance level.

3. *If the F-test is significant (p-value <0.05) that means that all the groups we are comparing differ from one another, doesn't it?* Not necessarily. A significant F-test could result from all the groups of the independent variable differing from one another, but it could also be that just one

▶

of the groups differs from the other two. For example, if we found a difference between black African, black Caribbean and white pupils, it could be that all three groups differ, or that black Caribbean students differ from the other two groups, or that white students differ from the other two groups, or that black African students differ from the other two groups. To know which groups actually differ, we need to do a post hoc test like the Scheffe test.

4. *Whenever we want to use nominal or ordinal independent variables, we must use ANOVA rather than regression.* That is not necessary. We can use ordinal and nominal (using dummy) independent variables in regression as well.

5. *An interaction effect gives us the combined effect of two variables on the dependent variable.* No, what interaction effects actually look at is whether or not the relationship between the dependent and independent variables differs for different groups of a third variable. For example, if we find a relationship between attitudes to school and achievement, could it be that this relationship exists for girls but not for boys?

■ ■ ■ Summary

In this chapter we looked at how we can compare the mean score of a continuous (or ordinal with many scale points) variable between a number of groups. The method we use to do this is called analysis of variance (ANOVA).

Like regression, ANOVA can look at the relationship between several independent variables and one continuous dependent variable. In contrast to regression, the independent variables in ANOVA have to be nominal or ordinal with a limited number of categories.

ANOVA will calculate both how well all the variables together predict the dependent variable (using the F-test and R square), and whether or not the individual variables are related to the dependent variable (using the F-test for statistical significance and the eta measure of effect size).

In order to see exactly which of the groups we are comparing differ from each other (e.g. treatment 1, treatment 2 and control) we need to calculate a post hoc test like the Scheffe test.

■ ■ ■ Exercises

1. You want to find out what factors predict achievement in English. Develop a model that you think can explain this.

2. Calculate your model using ANOVA (remember this limits what variables you can use). Does your model predict grades in English? How strongly does it predict English grades?

3. Calculate your model using ANOVA. Which individual variables predict English grades? How strong is their effect?

4. Calculate your model using ANOVA. Are there any interaction effects? What do they mean?

5. Calculate your model using ANOVA. What do the post hoc tests tell you?

6. Can you think of any arguments why you would want to use ANOVA rather than regression?

■ ■ ■ Further reading

As with regression, ANOVA will be discussed in pretty much all introductory textbooks.

Pedhazur, E. J. and Pedhazur Schmelkin, L. (1998) *Measurement Design and Analysis* (Lawrence Erlbaum) gives an excellent and extensive discussion of both regression and ANOVA.

Rutherford, A. (2001) *Introducing ANOVA and ANCOVA: A GLM Approach* (Sage) gives a good overview of the technique and its extension, analysis of co-variance (ANCOVA).

Turner, J. and Thayer, J. (2001) *Introduction to Analysis of Variance: Design, Analysis and Interpretation* (Sage) is an introduction aimed at producing a solid understanding of the method by using a calculator rather than a software package.

■■■ Chapter 11

One step beyond: introduction to multilevel modelling and structural equation modelling

In this chapter we will introduce some of the more advanced statistics which can help us solve some of the problems we have encountered with traditional methods so far. While it is not the goal of this book to provide a full treatment of these advanced methods, I think it is useful to introduce them. This will allow you both to interpret studies that have used these methods and point you in the right direction if you want to extend your knowledge of quantitative methods in future.

One thing to point out here is that both the methods that we will be looking at are essentially extensions of multiple regression analysis, which we discussed in Chapter 9. This once again points to the versatility and usefulness of this method. It also suggests that you should try and get a good understanding of regression (for example, by reading some of the books suggested in Chapter 9) before you start using these techniques.

■■■ Multilevel modelling

Why use multilevel modelling?

Another extension of regression modelling, and one that is particularly important in education, is *multilevel modelling*. Multilevel modelling is in many ways very similar to multiple regression, in that it is also used to look at the relationship between a dependent variable (usually continuous, although it is possible to develop multilevel versions of logit and probit regression as well), and one or (usually) more predictor variables. If multilevel analysis essentially does the same thing as regression, why are we bothering with it?

There are two main reasons. One is statistical, the other more substantive and related to fundamental research questions we might want to ask.

The statistical reason is related to sampling. Multiple linear regression (along with most related methods) assumes that we have a random sample from the population of interest. This means that if, as in the dataset we have been using in this book, we want to look at the relationship between pupils' self-concept and achievement with the intention of generalising our findings to the population of children of that age group nationally, we would have to randomly sample pupils from the whole of the country. This would mean that we would have to pick a very large number of names of children in Year 4 out of a hat (or more likely out of a computer). This hardly ever happens in educational research, as it would mean that we could end up with 900 pupils in something like 880 different schools! This would have obvious cost implications and mean that we could not be able to say anything about the effect of schools, classrooms or teachers. After all, if we have only one child in a particular school, that hardly allows us to say anything about children in that school more generally!

Therefore we usually sample schools (or even LEAs), and look at all or a sample of pupils in those schools. This means we no longer have a random sample. What we now have is a *hierarchical* or *cluster* sample. In that kind of sample, pupils are *nested* in schools.

This of course may, and usually in educational research will, mean that we are faced with a situation in which pupils within a school or classroom are more similar to one another on a variety of characteristics than they are to the sample as a whole. One reason for this is that school catchment areas tend to be more homogeneous in terms of social class than society as a whole. The social background of pupils within a school is therefore more similar than that of pupils nationally. Also, the fact that pupils are in a particular school means that they influence one another, and that they are all influenced by the culture of the school they are in. In research we often find that tastes in music, TV programmes and clothing are more similar within school than you would expect by chance because of the way kids influence one another. The same would go for other hierarchical samples. If we sample companies, and interview all employees within a company, these again are likely to be more similar to one another on a variety of characteristics than are employees in the general population.

This has an important statistical consequence. Whenever we have clustered samples it means that if we just use multiple linear regression and pretend we have a random sample, we will probably be underestimating the extent of standard error of the variance (the standard deviation of the predicted true value for a given observed value). Does this really matter? Yes, as this will lead to the effect of certain predictor variables wrongly being classified as statistically significant.

The second reason to use MLM is substantive. Often in educational research we are interested in finding out about certain characteristics of

■ ■ ■ Underestimating standard errors: an example

That using multiple regression instead of multilevel modelling when we have clustered samples matters can be illustrated by the following example from my own research. In a study I did as part of my doctoral dissertation, I wanted to see whether pupils' media use affected their achievement at school. To do this, I asked pupils about the amount of television they watched, how much they played computer games and so on. I also collected data on variables such as parental education, prior achievement and pupils' self-concept.

The sample I used was a random sample of primary schools in which I surveyed all the pupils in Year 4. Therefore, it is a cluster sample, with pupils nested within schools.

I first analysed the data using multiple regression and found that, controlling for the parental background variables and self-concept, there was a weak but statistically significant relationship between the amount of time pupils spent watching TV and playing computer games, and their achievement. The relationship was negative, so the more they watched, the lower their test scores. The same was true of computer game playing.

I then re-analysed the same data using multilevel modelling. Once I had done that, the effect of the two media variables became insignificant! It is clear then that the use of multiple regression rather than multilevel modelling can have substantive consequences.

schools and classrooms, and how they relate to pupil characteristics. For example, we might want to know whether what teachers do in the classroom (how they interact with pupils or what teaching style they have) affects pupils' performance. What multilevel modelling allows us to do is to look at how much of the variance in pupils' achievement is explained at the individual level, how much at the classroom level and how much at the school level, for example.

An example of multilevel modelling in practice

I will give another example of my own research to illustrate this. As part of an evaluation, Professor David Reynolds and myself analysed the effect of school (e.g. school social mix), classroom (e.g. teacher behaviours) and pupil background factors (e.g. eligibility for free lunch) on primary pupils' progress in mathematics, using a hierarchical sample (see Muijs and Reynolds, 2000). We gave pupils a maths test at the start of the school year and again at the end of the school year, and used multilevel modelling to look a how much their scores had changed over the year. The results are given in Table 11.1 which is a typical multilevel modelling output table. Our dependent variable is end-of-year test scores. Our predictor in this model is beginning-of-year test scores.

In Table 11.1 we can see the predictor variables listed under 'Variable'. Here, these are a 'constant' and 'beginning-of-year test scores'. The constant is the intercept, just like in multiple regression, and does not have a strong substantive meaning. The coefficients are similar to our bs in multiple regression and are interpreted in the same way. So, as the coefficient for beginning-of-year test scores is 0.86, our model predicts that if a child's beginning-of-year test score goes up by 1, her end-of-year test scores are predicted to go up by 0.86. The number in brackets is the standard error. If the coefficient is *more than twice as large as the standard error*, the relationship is statistically significant at the 0.05 level. Here, the coefficient (b = 0.86) is 43 times larger than the standard error (0.02), so the relationship is highly significant.

The next part of the output is called 'level'. This will tell us how much of the unexplained variance in pupil achievement (once the effect of beginning-of-year test scores is taken into account) is due to differences between the individual pupils, due to the fact that pupils attend different

▓ **Table 11.1** Multilevel model: end-of-year test scores predicted by beginning-of-year test scores

	Coefficients	% variance to be explained
Variable:		
Constant	16.97 (1.87)	
Beginning-of-year test score	0.86 (0.02)	
Level:		
School	4.18 (1.34)	2.7%
Class	14.62 (2.00)	9.6%
Pupil	134.11 (3.65)	87.7%

classrooms, or due to the fact that pupils attend different schools. The first number is again the coefficient, the amount of variance to be explained at that level. The number between brackets is the standard error. The same rule of thumb (coefficient needs to be at least twice the standard error) can be used to determine whether the relationship is statistically significant. Here, all three levels are statistically significant. As the coefficients in themselves don't mean that much, we usually convert them into percentages. These are given in the final column. As you can see, most of the variance (87.7 per cent) is due to individual differences between pupils, with a smaller (but significant) percentage being due to the fact that pupils go to different schools and classrooms.

In the next step, we are going to add some variables that might explain some of the differences between individual pupils (see Table 11.2).

In the column under 'variable', we can now see the names of the three variables we have added: special needs (does the child have special needs on a scale from 1 to 5), eligible for free school meals (is the child eligible for free school meals or not – this is a dummy variable) and gender. In the next column we can once again see the coefficients and the standard errors. Special needs and free school meal eligibility both have coefficients more than twice as large as the standard error (in brackets) and are therefore statistically significant predictors of the outcome. Gender does

■ **Table 11.2** Multilevel model: end-of year test scores predicted by beginning-of-year test scores and pupil variables

	Coefficients	% variance to be explained	Variance explained
Variable:			
Constant	26.18 (6.88)		
Beginning-of-year test score	0.80 (0.02)		
Special needs	–2.93 (0.59)		
Eligible for free school meals	–0.15 (0.02)		
Gender	–0.13 (0.44)		
Level:			
School	3.98 (1.59)	3.2%	4.8%
Class	12.43 (2.09)	9.9%	14.9%
Pupil	109.29 (3.51)	86.9%	18.5%

not. If we look at the dummy variable free school meals as an example, we can see that the coefficient for this variable is –0.15. This means that pupils with free school meal eligibility (the poorer pupils) are predicted to have a score that is 0.15 lower on the end-of-year test.

Under 'levels' we can again see the variance explained at the three levels. We can see that in all cases this variance has decreased compared to Table 11.1. For example, variance to be explained at the pupil level has gone down from 134.11 to 109.29. In the last column, this has been converted to a percentage (18.5). This means that the three variables we have introduced have explained 18.5 per cent of the variance between individual pupils. Or, put another way, part of the reason for the fact that individual pupils perform differently on the end-of year test can be explained by whether or not they have special needs and whether or not they are eligible for free meals. We can also see that, notwithstanding the fact that these variables are measured at the individual pupil level, they also explain variance at the school and classroom levels (4.8 per cent and 14.9 per cent respectively). This suggests that schools (due to their catchment area) and classrooms (probably due to the fact that some of these schools set pupils by ability) are somewhat homogeneous with respect to these pupil variables.

Finally, we will introduce some school and classroom variables to see whether those can explain some more variance. The variables are teaching quality (as measured through classroom observation), class size and whether or not the school sets pupils by ability (see Table 11.3).

We can now look at the coefficients for the three new variables in the same way. We can see that neither class size or setting have a coefficient that is more than twice as large as the standard error (between brackets) and so are not statistically significant. Teaching quality is. The coefficient of 0.52 suggests that an increase of 1 on the teaching quality scale is predicted to lead to an increase of 0.52 in end-of-year test scores. If we

■ **Table 11.3** Multilevel model: end-of-year test scores predicted by beginning-of-year test scores, pupil, school and classroom variables

	Coefficients	% variance to be explained	Variance explained
Variable:			
Constant	22.83 (6.88)		
Beginning-of-year test score	0.79 (0.02)		
Special Needs	−2.85 (0.59)		
Eligible for free school meals	−0.14 (0.02)		
Gender	−0.11 (0.43)		
Class size	0.05 (0.08)		
Setting (yes or no)	0.32 (0.83)		
Teaching quality	0.52 (0.15)		
Level:			
School	2.51 (0.94)	2.2%	36.9%
Class	2.94 (1.04)	2.6%	76.3%
Pupil	108.43 (3.48)	95.2%	0.9%

look at the variance for the three levels, we can see that these variables have explained most of the remaining variance at the classroom level (so teaching quality, as that is the main variable here, explains most of the differences between children's scores that result from them attending different classes), some of the differences at the school level and hardly any of the differences at the individual pupil level.

This example shows that multilevel modelling is useful in telling us more about how our variables are related to one another. We can see that, for example, most of the differences between how pupils perform is explained by individual differences between pupils rather than school or classroom factors. School and classroom factors are significant, however, and can largely be explained by differences in teaching quality.

■ ■ ■ How to do multilevel modelling

While SPSS has now introduced a multilevel modelling add-in, it is fair to say that multilevel modelling is still best done by using one of the statistical packages designed specifically for this. The two most commonly used are HLM (available from Scientific Software International (www.ssicentral.com)) and MLWin (available from London University's Institute of Education (www.ioe.ac.uk/mlwin)). Both have advantages and disadvantages, but both are flexible and reasonably user-friendly. The multi-purpose statistical analysis programme SAS also allows you to do multilevel modelling.

■ ■ ■ Structural equation modelling

Why use structural equation modelling?

Another method that is being used increasingly in quantitative educational research is *structural equation modelling* (SEM). Like multilevel modelling, it advances the discipline further by solving both substantive and statistical problems that the traditional methods we discussed earlier cannot handle. Like multilevel modelling, SEM is based on principles used in regression analysis.

A major substantive issue concerns the model we are using to relate our dependent variable to our predictors. In both multiple regression and multilevel modelling we are basically saying that all our predictors have a direct effect on the dependent variable. We might, for example, want to look at whether or not we can predict achievement at the end of the school year (achievement time 2) by prior achievement (beginning of year or time 1), parental background (low SES being related to lower achievement), pupil self-concept (lower self-concept being related to lower achievement) and pupil media use (higher use of the media, e.g. television, being related to lower achievement). Figure 11.1 illustrates the model of causal relationships we are using whenever we choose to employ multiple linear regression.

Theoretically, this might well not be the model we are hypothesising. Our prior research and theorising may make us prefer a more complex model than the one depicted in Figure 11.1. We might hypothesise a number of direct effects (e.g. social background on achievement at time 2) as well as a number of indirect effects (for example, parental social background may affect achievement at time 1, which may in turn affect pupil self-concept, which in turn has an effect on achievement at time 2). This may give us a model that looks more like the one depicted in Figure 11.2.

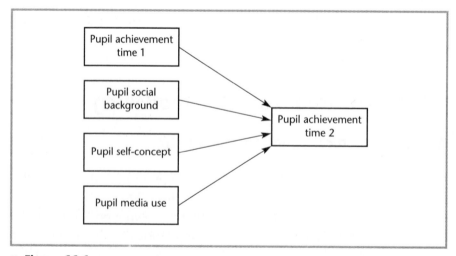

▓ **Figure 11.1**
Predictors of achievement: a regression model.

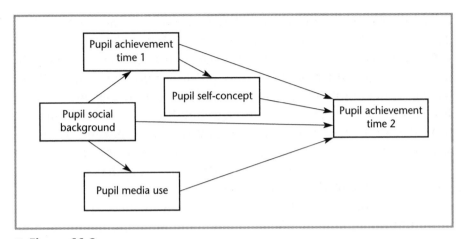

■ **Figure 11.2**
A more complex model.

Obviously, it would be interesting to test a model like that, as most of our theoretical models in education are likely to look more like the one shown in Figure 11.2 than the one shown in Figure 11.1, because of the complexity of the field. That is exactly what we can do in structural equation modelling.

Another reason we use structural equation modelling has to do with the issue of measurement error. As you know, whenever we measure anything in education and the social sciences more generally, we do this with a certain amount of error. Our measurement instruments are imperfect, and human beings are somewhat unpredictable. Therefore, as we saw in Chapter 4, whenever we measure something like self-concept (using a questionnaire item for example), the scores we get for each pupil will contain two elements: the 'true' score and the measurement error. As we discussed in Chapter 4, we want our measurement error to be as small as possible. Nevertheless, some measurement error always remains. In our standard regression procedures, we basically ignore this element and pretend that our scores are accurate. In structural equation modelling we can go one better and actually take the measurement error into account in our analyses.

This is where the concept of *latent variables* comes in. While we haven't discussed latent variables so far because they are not used as such in traditional quantitative methods like the ones we have discussed, this is another key concept, as you will see. The underlying idea behind the concept of latent variables is that most of the time we cannot, in the social sciences, directly measure what we want to measure. Think, for example of pupil self-concept. This is in essence an inner state of the person we are researching. We cannot directly 'look into people's minds' to get at their self-concept (and this is leaving aside the question of the extent to which such a thing actually exists or is brought into being by us researching it). Instead, we use questions or rating scales to try and measure this inner state. Each such question or rating scale we call a *manifest variable*. This is what we are actually measuring (for example, answers to the four questions on pupils' self-concept in mathematics in our dataset). We are, as researchers, not necessarily directly interested in these specific items though. What we actually want to know about is the latent variable, self-concept. What we can do in structural equation modelling that we can't do in multiple regression is look at the relationship between the latent rather than the manifest variables. How do we do this? Well, we tell the software program we are using to do the structural equation modelling that we are going to make a new variable, for example self-concept in mathematics (this is not a variable that we have actually measured in our questionnaire). Then we tell it that this item is made up of four manifest variables (variables we have actually measured in our questionnaire – see Figure 11.3).

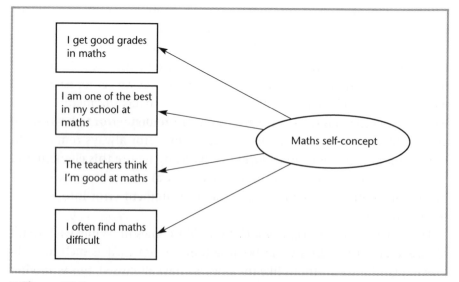

■ **Figure 11.3**
Four manifest variables determined by a latent maths self-concept.

The SEM program will then tell us whether these four manifest variables do indeed form a latent variable by giving us the fit of this model to the data. It will also be able to partial out the measurement error to a reasonable extent by looking at the relationship between the manifest variables and the latent variable. This method is called *confirmatory factor analysis* and is one part of SEM.

As mentioned above, SEM is an extension of multiple regression. Like multiple regression it will provide us with both coefficients telling us how much Y would change if X increased by 1 (e.g. in our model above, how much achievement at time 1 would go up by if the measure of parental background went up by 1), and a measure of how well the model fits the data. The former are given by the regression coefficients or bs. The second, the measure of overall fit to the data, is given by the chi square test (remember we encountered the chi square test in Chapter 6). There is one important difference between the chi square test as we used it earlier and as we use it here: in order for us to say that the model we have designed fits our data, chi square has to be *non-significant, or >0.05!* This is the opposite to the way of thinking we have had in all the rest of this book and so is a bit confusing, but that's statistics for you! There is a problem with chi square in that with these complex models it is very sensitive to sample size. If our sample is large enough it will detect even very small divergences of our model from the data, and models tested with large sample sizes almost never fit the data. Therefore a variety of fit indices have been developed that are less sensitive to sample size and are now more commonly used to look at whether our model fits the data. We will discuss a few of these below.

An example of the use of structural equation modelling

As part of the aforementioned study I was doing of primary mathematics teaching with Professor David Reynolds, we wanted to look at the extent to which teacher behaviours were related to pupil outcomes at the end of the year. We gave pupils a written and a verbal test at the beginning and end of the year, and observed over 100 lessons in our sample schools. We also wanted to find out about the teachers' behaviours. Using a rating scale like the ones discussed in Chapter 3, we measured teachers' behaviour in the areas of interaction with students, direct instruction, behaviour management, classroom management, varied teaching, individual review and practice and classroom climate. We hypothesised that all these manifest variables would form a 'global effective teaching' factor which was our latent variable. We also looked at the amount of time teachers spent teaching the whole class (in an interactive way) as opposed to allowing pupils to work on their own or in groups. These manifest variables were used to construct a latent variable called 'whole class interactive teaching', the teaching method the English government was promoting in primary mathematics at the time. Every five minutes we counted the number of pupils on and off task, and constructed a 'time on task' variable by calculating the total percentage of time pupils were on or off task.

In Figure 11.4, the manifest variables are depicted as squares while the latent variables are circles. As you can see, scores on the manifest variables are hypothesised to be determined by the latent variables. Latent variables in turn affect one another. The numbers next to the arrows are the standardised coefficients, or betas, like the ones we discussed in Chapter 9 on regression analysis (we can get the software to provide us with both the unstandardised bs, and standardised betas). If they are in italics the betas are statistically significant. So, we can see that our standardised regression coefficient for the relationship between September and July achievement is 0.83 and is statistically significant, while that for effective teaching behaviours is also statistically significant but, at 0.17, weaker than that for prior achievement.

Does our overall model fit the data? As I mentioned earlier, we will have to look at some fit indices to find out. Our chi square test is significant. This means that our model does *not* fit the data. However, we do have a large sample (over 2,000 pupils), so that might be causing the lack of fit. Because we have a large sample, we will look at some of the alternative fit indices I mentioned earlier that have been designed to be less sensitive to sample size. Three indices that we can look at are the goodness of fit index (GFI), the comparative fit index (CFI), and the root mean square error of approximation (RMSEA). All are calculated in a different way (it goes beyond this book to discuss those different methods here), and it is good practice to look at a number of different indices to see whether they contradict or confirm one another. As a rule of thumb, we say our model fits the data well if the GFI and CFI, which both vary between 0 and 1, are above 0.95, and if RMSEA is *below* 0.05. In this case, GFI was 0.99, CFI 0.98 and RMSEA 0.04. This suggests that our model fits the data well.

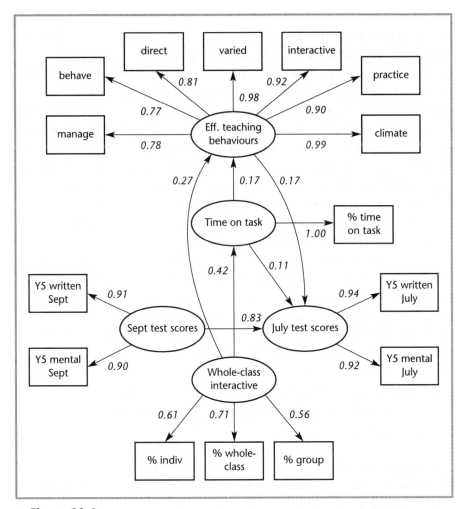

■ **Figure 11.4**
Year 5 structural equation model (significant paths in italics; completely standardised results).

The conclusion that we can draw is that our hypothesised model is not rejected. Prior achievement is the key determinant of end-of-year achievement. But teaching also matters: more time spent teaching the whole class interactively leads to higher levels of on-task behaviours and allows teachers to engage in more effective behaviours. These two factors in turn lead to higher achievement. However, some important caveats need to be taken into account: firstly, our model can only test those variables we have collected. There may be variables that we have not included that are more influential than those that we have included. Also, one important thing we need to take into account is that while this model is not rejected by the data, there may be equivalent models which fit the data equally well. For example, it may be that rather than teacher behaviours leading to higher achievement it is the case that teachers are able to perform better when they are teaching a high achieving class. Only if we replicate our model, and do not find any other models that fit the data as well or better, can we be totally confident of our findings. Also, in this example we have once again got a hierarchical sample (pupils in classrooms), so because we have not used multilevel modelling we might be overestimating the significance of our relationships. While attempts are ongoing to merge these two useful methods, at present this is still quite difficult to do with real data.

As you can see, structural equation modelling is an extremely useful tool, which allows us to model the complex realities of educational research better than traditional techniques. It is always worth remembering, though, that however sophisticated our analysis methods become, the results will only ever be as good as the data we have collected. In that sense, the first part of this book remains the most important one.

■ ■ ■ How to use structural equation modelling

Like multilevel modelling, structural equation modelling is currently best done with specifically designed software packages, of which there are a number on the market.

The most user-friendly package is probably AMOS, and this would be a good place to start for most users. It is not the most versatile, however. LISREL (available from SSIcentral.com) and EQS are the oldest programs on the market. Both combine reasonably user-friendly interfaces with broad functionality. The newest kid on the block is Mplus (www.muthen.com). This program is the best one to use if you have non-standard data, or if you want to explore advanced applications like multilevel structural equation modelling. It is not the most user-friendly, however, and probably not for the beginning user.

■ ■ ■ Summary

In this chapter we have given a brief introduction to two of the more recent and more advanced statistical methods used in educational research. Both are extensions of multiple regression.

Multilevel modelling was designed for use with hierarchical or cluster samples. It allows us to look at the amount of variance to be explained at the different levels (schools, classrooms, individual pupils, for example) at which the variance in the outcome measure can be explained. We were able to find out, for example, that almost 88 per cent of the variance in pupil outcomes could be explained by differences between individual pupils, with the rest being attributable to the fact that these pupils went to different schools or classrooms.

Structural equation modelling allows us to look at more complex models than traditional or multilevel modelling techniques. Rather than just hypothesising that all the individual variables directly affect the outcome variable, we can model indirect effects as well. Structural equation modelling also allows us to distinguish manifest variables (the variables we have actually measured) from latent variables (the concepts we are actually trying to measure and of which the manifest variables are the indicators).

■ ■ ■ Common misconceptions

1. *We use multilevel modelling to solve problems we get if we don't have a random sample, don't we?* In part. Multilevel modelling will solve some of the problems we get if we have used cluster sampling (we sample schools and survey all pupils in those schools, for example) rather than random sampling. It will not solve problems of bias inherent in other sampling methods like convenience sampling, though.

2. *If a level only explains a small percentage of the variance, that means it is unimportant, doesn't it?* Not necessarily. A small percentage of variance explained, like the 12 per cent we found in our sample for the school and classroom levels, can still make a substantive difference in practice. We found in that sample that the predicted difference between the test scores of pupils taught in the most as opposed to the least effective classroom was as high as 20 per cent.

▶

3. *If we don't use multilevel modelling when we have a hierarchical sample, we will underestimate the significance of our variables, won't we?* No, what will happen is that we will underestimate our standard errors. This will lead to us overestimating the significance of our relationships. In some cases, we might wrongly conclude that a relationship is statistically significant at the 0.05 level when in fact it isn't. Do remember that significance levels are arbitrary cut-off points, however.

4. *In structural equation models, if our chi square is significant (less than 0.05), that means that our model fits the data, doesn't it?* No, I'm afraid it is the other way round. Our model fits the data if chi square is non-significant (>0.05). I know this is a bit confusing, as it is the other way round from what we usually do.

5. *If my model fits the data, that means that we can accept it, right?* Not really. Our model is only tested on the variables we have measured. We may have left out a crucial variable that we have not collected in our study. Also, another model may fit our data just as well (or better) than the one we have constructed. Only if we can replicate our model over time and find that it keeps fitting can we be completely confident that it is true.

6. *A latent variable is a variable that we have not yet included in our model, isn't it?* No. The latent variable is the concept that we want to explore but haven't actually measured. For example, pupil attitudes to school would be a latent variable that we can measure by asking pupils whether they agree or disagree with a number of statements such as 'I like going to school'. These statements are our manifest variables.

■ ■ ■ Exercises

1. What are the main differences between multilevel modelling and multiple regression?
2. What are the main differences between structural equation modelling and multiple regression?
3. What are the main differences between multilevel modelling and structural equation modelling?

4. Can you think of a hypothesis or model you could test using structural equation modelling?

5. Can you think of a study for which you would use multilevel modelling?

6. Why do you think it might be useful to combine multilevel modelling and structural equation modelling?

■ ■ ■ Further reading

Obviously, we have only given a very cursory overview of the methods covered in this chapter. If you wanted to start using them you would have to do quite a bit of further reading. Luckily, accessible introductions exist to both multilevel modelling and structural equation modelling.

For multilevel modelling, a good place to start would be Heck, R. H. and Thomas, S. L. (1999) *An Introduction to Multilevel Modelling Techniques* (Lawrence Erlbaum). This is a user-friendly but comprehensive introduction to the subject while another good introductory text is Snijders, T. and Boskers, R. (1999) *Multilevel Analysis* (Altamira).

For those of you with a strong mathematical background, Goldstein, H. (2002) *Multilevel Statistical Models* (Edward Arnold) is one of the classic works on the subject. This is a mathematical introduction and not for the faint-hearted, however!

Structural equation modelling is blessed with an even greater number of introductory texts. Depending on which software you were thinking of using, Barbary Byrne's books *Structural Equation Modelling with AMOS* (2001), *Structural Equation Modelling with EQS* (1994) and *Structural Equation Modelling with LISREL* (1998) (all Lawrence Erlbaum) are all excellent and user-friendly introductions based around specific software packages.

Another good introductory text is Maruyama, G. (1997) *Basics of Structural Equation Modeling* (Sage). For more advanced users, Kaplan, D. (2000) *Structural Equation Modeling. Foundation and Extensions* (Sage) is an excellent book.

■ ■ ■ References

Aliaga, M. and Gunderson, B. (2002) *Interactive Statistics*. [Thousand Oaks]: Sage.

Byrne, B. M. and Shavelson, R. J. (1986) 'On the structure of adolescent self-concept', *Journal of Educational Psychology*, 78(6), 473–81.

Harris, A. (2001) 'Departmental improvement and school improvement: a missing link?', *British Journal of Educational Research*, 27(4), 477–86.

Johnson, J., Jackson, L. and Gatto, L. (1995) 'Violent attitudes and deferred academic aspirations: deleterious effects of exposure to rap music', *Basic and Applied Social Psychology*, 16(1/2), 27–41.

Lowry, R. (2002) *Some Basic Statistical Concepts and Methods for the Introductory Psychology Course Part 8*. Available at: http://faculty.vassar.edu/lowry/qm8.html.

Mayer, R. E. and Moreno, R. A. (1998) 'Split-attention effect in multimedia learning: evidence for dual processing systems in working memory', *Journal of Educational Psychology*, 90(2), 312–20.

Mulaik, S. A. (1995) 'The metaphoric origins of objectivity, subjectivity and consciousness in the direct perception of reality', *Philosophy of Science*, 62, 283–303.

Muijs, R.D. (1997) *Self, School and Media*. Leuven: Catholic University of Leuven, Department of Communication Science.

Muijs, R. D. (forthcoming) 'Measuring teacher effectiveness', in Hopkins, D. and Reynolds, D. (eds), *The Learning Level*. London: Routledge Falmer.

Muijs, R. D., and Reynolds, D. (2000) 'School effectiveness and teacher effectiveness: some preliminary findings from the evaluation of the mathematics enhancement programme', *School Effectiveness and School Improvement*, 11(3), 247–63.

Muijs, R. D. and Reynolds, D. (2002) 'Teacher beliefs and behaviors: what matters', *Journal of Classroom Interaction*, 37(2), 3–15.

Opdenakker, M.-C. and Van Damme, J. (2000) 'Effects of schools, teaching staff and classes on achievement and well-being in secondary education: similarities and differences between school outcomes', *School Effectiveness and School Improvement*, 11(2), 165–96.

Shavelson, R. J. (1976) 'Self-concept: validation of construct interpretations', *Review of Educational Research*, 46(3), 407–41.

Veenman, S., Bakermans, J., Franzen, Y. and Van Hoof, M. (1996) 'Implementation effects of a pre-service training course for secondary education teachers', *Educational Studies*, 22(2), 225–43.

■ ■ ■ Index

Added to the page number 'f' denotes a figure and 't' denotes a table.